EVOLVED FOREX TRADING.

A step-by-step guide to FOREX Trading.
Written and published by Oleg But.

Copyright © Oleg But and Adam Burgoyne, 2011

Edition revised, updated and new material added, 2011

Co-author Adam Burgoyne.
Cover design and artwork by Carina Zhiteneva.
Prepared for publication by Michael Owen.

ISBN-13: 978-1468108835

ISBN-10: 1468108832

Published in printed format and in electronic format

Evolved FOREX Trading

Step-by-step guide to FOREX trading with many explanatory illustrations. It is intended both for beginners and advanced FOREX traders, allowing you to master several excellent trading systems and approaches.

Oleg But

and Adam Burgoyne

Revised and New Material Added September 2011

Table of Contents

About This Book

This book is a step-by-step guide to FOREX trading with many explanatory illustrations. It is intended both for beginners and advanced FOREX traders, allowing you to master several excellent trading systems and approaches, such as day-trading, scalping and break-out systems, plus lots of "tips & tricks".

The book starts with basic concepts of the FOREX market and moves on to show you how to use technical indicators correctly, before explaining our FOREX trading systems (which include documented proof!)

Visit our website to view trading statements from our own accounts and those of other traders who are using our strategies: **www.evolvedforextrading.com**.

Currency

Unless otherwise stated in this book, all numbers preceded by the "$" sign refer to amounts in U.S. Dollars.

Updates

A video course will soon be available from our website so visit **www.evolvedforextrading.com** now and join our subscriber list to qualify for our "members" discount.

Disclaimer and Risk Warning

The terms "us", "we", "our", etc. hereto refer to Adam Burgoyne (co-author), Oleg But (author & publisher), their representatives and associates.

Trading any financial market involves risk.

The content of this e-book, its various associated websites and all related correspondence are neither a solicitation nor an offer to purchase of sell any financial instrument.

Although every attempt has been made to assure accuracy, we do not give any express or implied warranty as to its accuracy. We do not accept any liability for error or omission. Examples are only provided for illustrative and educational purposes and should not be construed as investment advice or strategy.

No representation is being made that any account or trader will or is likely to achieve profits or losses similar to those discussed in this e-book. Past performance is not indicative of future results.

By purchasing the e-book, subscribing to our mailing list or using our website in any way, you will be deemed to have accepted these terms in full.

We do not and cannot give investment advice.

Endeavors are made to insure that related websites are available 24 hours per day but no liability is accepted if, for any reason, a site is unavailable.

The information provided in this document is not intended for distribution to or for use by, any person or entity in any jurisdiction or country where such distribution or use would be contrary to law or regulation or which would subject us to any registration requirement within such jurisdiction or country.

Hypothetical performance results have many inherent limitations, some of which are mentioned below. No representation is being made that any account will or is likely to achieve profits or losses similar to those shown. In fact, there are frequently sharp differences between hypothetical performance results and actual results subsequently achieved by any particular trading program.

One of the limitations of hypothetical performance results is that they are generally prepared with the benefit of hindsight. Further, hypothetical trading does not involve financial risk, therefore, no hypothetical trading record can completely account for the impact of financial risk in actual trading.

For example: the ability to withstand losses or to adhere to a particular trading program in spite of trading losses are material points which can also adversely affect trading results. There are numerous other factors related to the market in general and to the implementation of any specific trading program, which cannot be fully accounted for in the preparation of hypothetical performance results, all of which can adversely affect actual trading results.

We reserve the right to change these terms and conditions without notice. You can check for updates to this disclaimer at any time without notification.

The content of this document, supplied software and all related websites and correspondence are copyright and may not be copied or reproduced.

U.S. Government Required Disclaimer

Commodity Futures Trading Commission Futures and Options trading have large potential rewards, but also large potential risk. You must be aware of the risks and be willing to accept them in order to invest in the FOREX, futures and options markets. The past performance of any trading system or methodology is not necessarily indicative of future results.

Dedications

I dedicate this book to my mother, Ludmila Aleksandrovna But. Although she understands nothing about trading the financial markets, she provides my motivation for success in this enchanting and exciting occupation. I wish her all my love and a long, happy, healthy life!

Oleg But

I dedicate this book to my wife, Zhanna, whose constant support made the uphill journey towards this point both possible and a reality.

Adam Burgoyne

Acknowledgments

I express my deepest gratitude to my good friend and co-author, Adam Burgoyne, for his help in the creation of this book and for his many tips regarding trading itself and trading systems development! I also thank him for bringing his software development expertise to the project! His FOREX trading and IT skills have been an immense help to me for a long time and, without him, this book would never have seen the light of day. I am extremely grateful for the gift of such an excellent, dependable friend!

Special thanks also go to Carina Zhiteneva, a very dear member of my family, for creating the cover for this book.

Finally, my thanks go to Michael Owen, not just for his tireless work on the layout and formatting of this book (which has made it so much more attractive and readable) but also for his continual assistance in all areas.

Oleg But

Evolved FOREX Trading

PART I

Preface to Part I

The **MAIN FOREX SYSTEM** actually consists of **two** trading systems: a *Day-Trading System* and a *Scalping System*.

In the **MAIN FOREX SYSTEM** we focus on the "Day-Trading" system: Our main goal is to earn 25-35 pips per day (*these and other terms which may be new to you are explained in some detail later in this book*).

A trading day in the FOREX market is 24 hours, which is why it is reasonable to refer to as a *Day-Trading* system. In fact, most FOREX trading systems can be considered to be *Day-Trading* systems.

A Day-Trading system has <u>one very important rule</u>: **you should not leave positions open overnight.** However, since the FOREX market is open from 17:00 EST (USA) Sunday through to 17:00 EST (USA) Friday, your own time zone makes "overnight" a subjective term.

In the FOREX market, "swaps" are calculated near the end of the trading day. We shall be learning about swaps later. One good reason not to leave a position open overnight – unless you thoroughly understand how they work and their impact on your trading account – is due to the calculation of negative swaps.

Although we refer to the primary method of the **MAIN FOREX SYSTEM** as "Day-Trading", with the flexibility to leave your positions open overnight, it could be called a short-term trading system, too. Regardless, we will consider it a Day-Trading system because:

Our **main goal** is for earning **25-35 pips per day** - we have 24 hours in which to do it! Our earlier comment: "with the flexibility to leave your positions open overnight", depends totally on market conditions at the time and whether your positions are in profit. At the end of the day, there is no reason not to leave a position open overnight if it is in profit and there is a strong trend in our direction.

CHAPTER 1
WHAT IS FOREX?

FOREX (FOReign EXchange Market)

The Foreign Exchange Market is the arena where a nation's currency is exchanged for that of another at a mutually agreed rate. The FOREX market was formed in the mid '70s, when international trade was changed from a system of fixed rates to a system of free-floating rates of exchange.

In fact, every country's currency is considered merchandise, like wheat or sugar; it is the same medium of exchange, like gold and silver. Since the world changes faster and faster every year, the economic conditions of every country (e.g. labor productivity, inflation, unemployment, etc.) are ever more dependant upon the level of development of other countries, and this, in turn, impacts the value of a country's currency in relation to the currencies of other countries. This is the main reason why there are rate fluctuations.

Currency Symbols:

EUR	Euro	**NZD**	New Zealand Dollar
USD	US Dollar	**SEK**	Swedish Krona
GBP	British Pound	**DKK**	Danish Kroner
JPY	Japanese Yen	**NOK**	Norwegian Kroner
CHF	Swiss Franc	**SGD**	Singapore Dollar
AUD	Australian Dollar	**ZAR**	South African Rand
CAD	Canadian Dollar		

Currency Exchange Rate

Currency exchange rates are simply the ratio of one currency valued against another. For example, "EUR/USD exchange rate is 1.2505" means that one euro is traded for 1.2505 dollars.

The exchange rate of any currency is usually given as a **bid** price (left) and an **ask** price (right).

The bid price represents what has to be obtained in the quote currency (US Dollar, in our example) when selling one unit of the base currency (Euro, in our example).

The ask price represents what has to be paid in the quote currency (US Dollar, in our example) to obtain one unit of the base currency (Euro, in our example).

The difference between the bid and the ask price is referred to as the **spread.**

Spread varies between currency pairs and also between brokers but, typically, the most liquid and heavily traded currency pairs will have spreads of 4 pips or less.

In this instance, let us assume the exchange rate for EUR/USD is: 1.2505/1.2509.

You may have done some market analysis and decide the EUR/USD rate is moving higher (at least to 1.2600) so you buy 0.1 lots (minimum contract size for a "standard" or "mini" account) of EUR/USD at the 1.2509 ask price.

Lot Sizes For Different Currency Pairs			
Currency	1.0 lot size	Req. margin for 1 lot	1 pip
EURUSD	EUR 100,000	1,000 EUR	0.0001
USDCHF	USD 100,000	1,000 USD	0.0001
GBPUSD	GBP 70,000	700 GBP	0.0001
USDJPY	USD 100,000	1,000 USD	0.01
AUDUSD	AUD 200,000	2,000 AUD	0.0001
USDCAD	USD 100,000	1,000 USD	0.0001
EURCHF	EUR 100,000	1,000 EUR	0.0001
EURJPY	EUR 100,000	1,000 EUR	0.01
EURGBP	EUR 100,000	1,000 EUR	0.0001
GBPJPY	GBP 70,000	700 GBP	0.01
GBPCHF	GBP 70,000	700 GBP	0.0001
EURCAD	EUR 100 000	1,000 EUR	0.0001
EURAUD	EUR 100 000	1,000 EUR	0.0001
NZDUSD	NZD 200,000	2,000 NZD	0.0001
USDSEK	USD 100,000	1,000 USD	0.0001
USDDKK	USD 100,000	1,000 USD	0.0001
USDNOK	USD 100,000	1,000 USD	0.0001
USDSGD	USD 100,000	1,000 USD	0.0001
USDZAR	USD 100,000	1,000 USD	0.0001
CHFJPY	CHF 100,000	1,000 CHF	0.01

The table above will help you identify what the contract size is, i.e. 1.0 lot for EUR/USD is 100,000 EUR so 0.1 lot (our contract size) is 10,000 EUR.

This means you bought 10,000 EUR and sold 10,000 * 1.2509 = 12,509 USD.

Now, in order to make a trade, you do not need to have the total amount of $12,509 available. You actually require just a fraction of that amount as the rest of the money is leveraged to you by a broker (a company you contracted with to enter the market).

Leverage

Leverage is the term used to describe margin requirements - the ratio between the collateral and borrowed funds.

This ratio will vary between brokers based on their internal policies and/or due to legislation but the most common options are 1:1, 1:20, 1:40, 1:50, 1:100, 1:200, 1:300, 1:400 and 1:500.

If your broker offers 1:100 leverage then opening a new position only requires a deposit of 1/100th of the contract size.

In our example on the previous page, the exchange rate was 1.2509 so, with 1:100 leverage, the margin (security deposit) required would equate to $125.09 meaning that $12,383.91 was being loaned to you by the broker.

It is important to understand that the margin required to open a position is immediately ring-fenced in your account when a position is opened and is not available to you until that position has been closed, at which point the broker releases the funds back to you.

Note: US brokers are legally restricted to 1:50 and 1:20 so finding a non-US broker is extremely advantageous if you have a small deposit amount. This is more difficult for US traders but our website includes details of brokers able to assist in this area.

How a Transaction Is Carried Out

So, you speculate that EUR/USD is moving higher and you buy 10,000 EUR and sell 12,509 USD.

Assuming that you are right and EUR/USD reaches 1.2599/1.2603, you close the open position with an opposing one.

In our example, you close the long (buy) position with a short (sell) position, i.e. you sell 10,000 EUR (0.1 lots * 1.0 lot size for EUR/USD) and buy 12,509 USD:

Transaction	EUR	USD
Open a position - buy EUR and sell USD	+ 10,000	- 12,509
Close a position - sell EUR and buy USD	- 10,000	+ 12,599
Total:	0	+ 90

You get a profit of 90 pips = $90 in this case. Importantly, you did not require 10,000 EUR ($12,509) to make the trade, just $125.

Note: A *Pip* or *point* is the minimum fluctuation in a currency rate. Some brokers quote rates to 4 decimal places (as we have done) and others quote to 5 decimals. Brokers quoting to 5 decimal places are said to be offering "fractional pricing" which has become the trend.

Fractional pricing is a mechanism designed to facilitate narrower spread offers which can make brokers seem more appealing to potential clients.

For example, a broker quoting to 4 decimal places and offering a spread of 1 pip on EUR/USD has no room to maneuver whereas a broker quoting to 5 decimal places and offering a spread of 10 pips can easily drop that to 9, 8, etc. (0.9, 0.8) to gain a marketing advantage over competitors.

For EUR/USD, 1 pip is 0.0001 of the price (see Table 2) so our profit in this example is 1.2599 - 1.2509 = 0.0090, i.e. 90 pips.

So, you invested $125 and made a profit of $90.

The time period to achieve this could be anywhere between a few seconds and several days. Assuming that it actually took a few hours, a profit of $90 for an investment of $125 and no actual "work" is not a bad return at all.

However, you must be aware that leverage can also work against you and magnify your losses.

Only money management will help you to minimize the risks, ideally reduce them to zero, and increase the return from your funds to 10%, 20%, 30% or higher each month.

One question is left: what is the broker's charge for the leverage they provide?

If you open and close a position before rollover (generally 23:00 GMT), brokers provide the leverage for free. If you leave your position open, they adjust your account with a storage charge for the overnight position. It can be either positive (credited to your account) or negative (debited to your account) depending upon the interest rates in those countries.

For example: ECB interest rate is 4.25%, FED interest rate is 3.5%. Assume you have a short position on EUR/USD of 1.0 lot so you have sold 100,000 EUR. This means you have borrowed them at 4.25% per annum.

You sold Euros and bought Dollars, which can be deposited at 3.5% per annum. As a result, the costs are (4.25% - 3.50%) per annum or $937.50 per year (if the EUR/USD rate is 1.2500), or $2.57 per day.

This means that your account will be debited with $2.57 every day for each lot if you have a short (selling) position on EUR/USD and credited with $2.57 if you have a long (buying) position.

In practice, the debited amount would be a little higher than $2.57 and the credited amount a little lower with the difference going to the broker to offset their costs.

Swaps

The following table includes examples of swap rates, expressed in pips. The actual values fluctuate based on the exchange rate of each currency and the interest rates of the countries involved at the time rollover is calculated

Symbol	Long	Short
EURUSD	-0.830 pips	0.580 pips
USDCHF	1.200 pips	-1.410 pips
GBPUSD	-0.110 pips	-0.170 pips
USDJPY	1.38 pips	-1.54 pips
AUDUSD	0.130 pips	-0.260 pips
USDCAD	0.230 pips	-0.400 pips
EURCHF	0.480 pips	-0.830 pips
EURJPY	0.780 pips	-1.060 pips
EURGBP	-0.490 pips	0.330 pips
GBPJPY	2.460 pips	-2.770 pips
GBPCHF	2.1400 pips	-2.540 pips
EURCAD	-0.580 pips	0.280 pips
EURAUD	-1.560 pips	1.180 pips
NZDUSD	0.520 pips	-0.630 pips
USDSEK	5.09 pips	-6.35 pips
USDDKK	3.11 pips	-4.31 pips
USDNOK	3.24 pips	-4.74 pips
USDSGD	0.480 pips	-0.78 pips
USDZAR	-6.22 pips	3.57 pips
CHFJPY	0.130 pips	-0.270 pips
GOLD	-3.50% per year	1.50% per year
CFD on stocks	-3.50% per year	1.50% per year
CFD on futures	-	-

Note: the storage charge for the rollover from Wednesday to

Thursday is **_three times higher_** than for a position held over any other night.

This is because, in the spot currency market, funds ordered when you open a position are not received until 2 business days after the position is opened and, by the same token, when closing a position, those funds are not returned for 2 business days.

This means that positions opened on Wednesday and closed on Thursday would result in receipt of funds on Friday which could not be returned until Monday, therefore incurring rollover charges for Friday, Saturday and Sunday nights. Sorry if that seemed overly complicated – it probably was!

The main thing you need to remember is that you will see a much larger rollover charge if you hold a position open over Wednesday night.

The Reasons for the Popularity of FOREX

In today's financial markets, whether you are a small or large investor, the Foreign Exchange Market (FOREX) is the most profitable sector for your investments.

Unlike other financial markets, the FOREX market has no physical location, like a stock exchange for example. Instead, it operates through the electronic network of banks, computer terminals and even the humble telephone.

The lack of any physical exchange enables the FOREX market to operate on a 24-hour basis, spanning one time zone to another across the major financial centers (Sydney, Tokyo, Hong Kong, Frankfurt, London, New York, etc).

In every financial center there are many dealers who buy and sell currencies 24 hours per day throughout the entire business week.

Each daily trading session starts in New Zealand (Wellington) then moves on to Sydney, Tokyo, Hong Kong, Singapore, Moscow, Frankfurt-on-Maine, London, New York and ends in Los Angeles.

The approximated trading hours for regional markets (New York Time) are:

Japan	07:00 PM-04:00 AM New York Time
Continental Europe	09:30 AM-16:00 PM New York Time
Great Britain	03:00 AM-12:00 PM New York Time
USA	08:00 AM-05:00 PM New York Time

Now, let us look at the most important reasons why FOREX is so popular today:

Liquidity

FOREX is the largest financial market in the world, with the equivalent of $3-4 trillion changing hands daily, whereas the volume of the stock markets is only around $500 billion.

Flexibility

Due to its 24-hour per day nature, participants of the Foreign Exchange Market do not have to wait for a reaction to certain external events in the same way as other daily markets (stock or futures markets, for example).

In these other markets, it is normal for prices at the "open" of the next day to "gap" up or down from the previous day's closing prices because, by morning of whatever time zone you are in, the opening price will have already factored in the impact of any relevant overnight events.

Depending upon your position, this may or may not be desirable so, generally speaking, you should aim to trade markets in your own time zone to avoid the situation. That is where the 24-hour aspect of FOREX is a great advantage.

Lower transaction costs

Traditionally, the FOREX market has no commissions (other than the spread - the difference between bid and ask prices).

Price stability

High liquidity helps ensure price stability when unlimited contract sizes can be executed at a fair price. It helps avoid the problem of instability, as happens in the stock market and other exchange-traded markets because of the lower trade volumes where, at any given price, only a limited number of contracts can be executed.

Margin

The margin requirement for trading on FOREX is defined in the contract entered into by a client and a bank or a brokerage company.

This provides an opportunity for individuals to enter the market easily - usually with a capital requirement of just 1% of the contract value.

That means collateral of just $1,000 can allow a trader to execute trades of $100,000.

Such high leverage, combined with the frequent and rapid rate fluctuations common in FOREX can make this market extremely profitable but at the same time extremely risky.

Classification Features of the FOREX Market

The FOREX market can be classified by its different features:

By type of operations

There is a World Market of conversion operations (consisting, for example, of conversion markets like US Dollar/Japanese Yen or US Dollar/Canadian Dollar, and so on).

By territorial feature

The International Currency Market (FOREX) is a system of markets associated with the assistance of modern technologies.

The most significant ones would be the Asiatic (Tokyo, Singapore, Hong Kong), European (London, Frankfurt on Maine, Zurich) and American (New York, Chicago, Los Angeles) markets.

It is also possible to indicate national currency markets (i.e. Russian currency market) with a wide complex of currency operations.

Due to the location of world regional markets in different time zones it is correct to say that the International Currency Market works around the clock.

It begins in the Far East, New Zealand (Wellington), passing time zones in Sidney, Tokyo, Hong Kong, Singapore, Moscow, Frankfurt on Maine, London and finishes the day in New York and Los Angeles.

CHAPTER 2
THE MAIN MARKET
PARTICIPANTS

The main currency market participants are:

Commercial banks

They hold the primary capacity of currency operations. Other market participants hold accounts with banks and use them to realize their required conversion and deposit-credit operations.

A bank accumulates (through its operations with clients) the combined market needs in terms of currency conversions and effects them with the help of other banks.

Besides simply fulfilling clients' requests, banks can also effect transactions on their own behalf. The result is a currency market made up of inter-bank deals.

In the world currency markets, prominent international banks create the main influence as the value of their everyday operations is huge. These banks are Deutsche Bank, Barclays Bank, Union Bank of Switzerland, Citibank, Chase Manhattan Bank, Standard Chartered Bank, etc.

Their main criterion is the prominent volume of their deals which can cause important changes in quotations or in the price of a currency.

Usually, these major players are subdivided into "bulls" and "bears".

Bulls are interested in increasing the price of a currency while bears are interested in lowering the price.

Usually, the market is in a relatively balanced condition between bulls and bears where the difference in currency quotation changes within rather tight limits.

When imbalance allows bulls or bears to dominate a currency, quotations change much faster.

Companies making foreign investments

These are those companies involved with Investment Funds, Money Market Funds and International Corporations.

These companies show constant demand for foreign currency (as importers) and offer foreign currency (as exporters). Also, they place spare funds on short-term deposit.

At the same time, companies with direct access to the currency market do not, as a rule, effect conversion and deposit operations through commercial banks.

These companies, represented by various international investment funds, operate a portfolio strategy for investment of assets, arranging funds in securities of the Governments of different countries. In dealers' slang they are referred to as *funds*, the most well-known of which are G. Soros' "Quantum", for successful currency speculations, and "Dean Witter".

Other types of companies that belong in this category are the great international corporations, creating foreign production investments: the creation of offices, combined business, etc. such as Xerox, Nestle, General Motors, British Petroleum and others.

Central banks

Their main task is currency regulation of their internal market - staving off sudden jumps in rate of a national currency to avoid economical crisis, maintaining a balance of import-export, etc.

Central banks have an influence on the currency market. Their influence could be direct – in the case of currency intervention, or indirect – through regulating the volume of money supply and bank rates.

They are not to be confused with bulls or bears, as their role involves the resolution of international financial issues being faced at a given moment.

A central bank could affect the market independently, to influence its national currency or, in co-ordination with other central banks to arrange a combined currency policy with the international market.

The banks with the most influence on world currency markets are: The United States (the US Federal Reserve or FED), Germany (Deutsche Bundesbank) and Great Britain (the Bank of England, the so-called "Old Lady").

Currency exchanges

Among some countries with transitive economies, there are currency exchanges which are there to both arrange exchanges and to formulate a market's rate of exchange. Their Governments usually regulate the level of rate of exchange.

Currency brokerages

Their function is to introduce a buyer to a foreign currency seller and effect a loan-deposit transaction. For this service, brokerage firms ask for a commission - usually as a percentage of the deal amount.

Private persons

Individuals arrange a wide spectrum of non-trade operations in the areas of foreign tourism, wages, pensions, fee transactions, buying/selling of cash currency, etc.

In 1983, with the creation of margined trades, the ability to invest spare funds in the FOREX market for profit became a viable option for individuals.

The majority of FOREX transactions (90-95%) are arranged by international commercial banks; their own transactions as well as those of their clients.

Advancements in computer technology within the financial sphere have opened the way for private and small investors as more brokerage firms and banks allow private investors to access FOREX via the Internet.

CHAPTER 3
THE MAIN CONCEPTS OF THE
FOREX MARKET

In banking practice there are special code abbreviations: for example, the exchange rate for the US Dollar against the Japanese Yen is referred to as USD/JPY and the British Pound against the US Dollar is referred to as GBP/USD.

The first currency is known as the **base currency** and the second as the **quote currency**:

Base currency	Quote currency		Rate
USD	JPY	=	120.25

This notation specifies how much you have to pay in the quote currency to obtain one unit of the base currency (in this example, 120.25 Japanese Yen for one US Dollar). The minimum rate fluctuation is called a **point** or **pip**.

Most currencies (except USD/JPY, EUR/JPY and GBP/JPY, where a pip is 0.01) use 4 decimal places, i.e. 0.0001. If your broker offers fractional pricing then one pip becomes 10x smaller i.e. 0.001 equates to one pip for the JPY currency pairs and 0.00001 equates to one pip for the other currency pairs.

The currency pairs on FOREX are quoted as **bid** and **ask** (or **offer**) prices:

Currency	Bid		Ask
USD / JPY =	120.25	/	120.30

Bid

Bid is the rate at which you can sell the base currency, in our case it is the US Dollar, and buy the quote currency, i.e. Japanese Yen.

Ask (or offer)

Ask (or offer) is the rate at which you can buy the base currency, in our case US Dollars, and sell the quote currency, i.e. Japanese Yen.

Spread

Spread is the difference between the "bid" and "ask" prices.

Margin trading

Margin trading assumes that FOREX dealing is based on the margin, the collateral, and the provided leverage.

Such credits are provided by the brokerage companies, in addition to their informational services, and make it possible for a trader to enter into positions larger than his/her account balance. This collateral is typically referred to as *margin*.

Margin

Margin is the sum of a guarantee pledge under which leverage is provided.

Leverage

Leverage is the term used to describe margin requirements. It is expressed as the ratio between the collateral and borrowed funds, i.e. 1:20, 1:40, 1:50, 1:100, 1:200, 1:300, 1:400, 1:500.

Leverage of 1:100 means that when you wish to open a new position you need just $1/100^{th}$ of the contract size in available capital.

Currency Rate

Currency Rate is the ratio of one currency valued against another. It depends on the demand and supply within a free market or a market restricted by a government or central bank.

Lot

Lot is a fixed standard amount of a given currency for the purpose of trading. Sometimes it is known as the **contract size**. The monetary value of 1.0 lot for each currency pair was shown in the "Lot Sizes For Different Currency Pairs" table in chapter 1.

Storage

Storage is the charge to rollover (hold) a position overnight. It can be either positive (credited) or negative (debited) to your account balance depending on the interest rates in the countries of the currencies you are trading.

CHAPTER 4
MINI-FOREX – FOREX TRADING
WITH $500 DEPOSIT

Many brokers provide their clients with the ability to trade mini-FOREX contracts where margin requirements are less than $100 because the contract sizes are smaller than standard contracts.

This means that the average person can trade currencies alongside those with $100,000+ trading accounts and earn proportionally the same returns.

To trade mini-FOREX, a trader simply specifies a smaller lot size, i.e. 0.1, 0.2, etc. (at any rate, less than 1.0 lot).

Until 2003, there was a difference in trading conditions between mini-FOREX and standard FOREX and a commission of $3.00 was charged for each mini-FOREX contract. In mid-2003, this practice ceased and there is now no difference between mini-FOREX and standard FOREX.

Keep these things in mind:

The FOREX market is an inter-bank market with a minimum trade size of $1,000,000. How then do $10,000 trades, representing mini-FOREX contracts, get represented in an inter-bank market?

For small deals, clients require a partner, i.e. a brokerage. If the brokerage has a large number of clients trading mini-FOREX then it is conceivable that they could combine those orders to create an inter-bank market contract.

On the other hand, a brokerage with just a few clients would never reach minimum contract requirements to place a trade into the market.

In these circumstances, a brokerage might decide to assume any potential liability in the hope that the majority of their clients would hold losing positions, i.e. the brokerage takes opposing positions to their own clients. If the client wins then the brokerage loses and vice-versa.

A brokerage in this situation may try to tip the balance in their favor by shifting the quotation when closing trades, etc. to create unplanned losses for their clients.

Of course, if the brokerage has been in existence for some time then they have most likely amassed a large client-bank of active traders so combining contracts to take actual positions in the inter-bank market would not be an issue for them.

In such a scenario, the brokerage is not interested in whether a client wins or loses as they will be earning the pip spread in either case.

In practice, the brokerage does care whether their clients win because winning traders become more confident, active and more profitable for the brokerage.

More recently, "micro" accounts have become popular. These allow you to open trades 10 times smaller than with "mini" accounts i.e. 0.01 lots.

Such accounts make it even easier for investors to enter the Forex market as the minimum account balance can be as little as $100.

A slight issue with these accounts is that very few are traded directly on the inter-bank market so there is a high chance that your broker is trading against you.

There certainly are brokers who are able to place such small trades into the market by aggregating them but they are few and far between.

CHAPTER 5
WHAT WE NEED TO ACCESS THE MARKET AND TRADE IT

We Need an Internet Connection

Actually, transactions can be carried out by telephone. Some brokerages insist on carrying out transactions by telephone if the volume of transactions exceeds certain limits and also acts as a fail-safe option because neither software nor internet access can be guaranteed to operate 100% of the time. In these situations, transactions can be opened or cancelled by telephone.

Of course, it is to your advantage when you can work via the Internet as it allows continuous communication with the market and high speed execution of orders.

For our purposes, the best option is high-speed Internet. Either DSL or Cable is perfectly adequate and a dial-up connection for emergency use is a good idea. Remember that dial-up is for unforeseen situations - we would not recommend it for normal use.

For added safety, we strongly suggest purchasing a good Uninterruptible Power Supply (UPS) in case of local power failure.

Ok! We have discussed what is required and or prudent for us to connect with the brokerage and we have protected ourselves against various unforeseen situations. Now we need to choose a brokerage or Dealing Center through which we can access the market and place our trades.

We Need a Brokerage

There are many brokerage offices offering access to the FOREX market.

Use the following criteria for choosing a brokerage who will give you the best level of service:

1. **Reliability**.

> It is necessary to find out how many years the given company has been working in this sphere of business and how many clients it has.

> The longer it has worked in this sphere of business, and the more clients it has, the better

2. **Quantity and quality of services**:

> Technical support service

> Facilities for funding and withdrawing from a trading account, etc. to meet your personal requirements

3. **Number of available currency pairs for trading**

4. **Most important**:

> Pay attention to the size of their spreads (each brokerage is free to set their own) and the speed & quality of order executions.

> Consider the functionality of the trading terminal offered. Download it, install it and study the documentation until you are totally comfortable with it

You should know your trading terminal so well that you can instantly find any tool or feature when required.

Most importantly, you should understand the various orders and the rules relating to their execution – for example: the multiplication table.

In this section we have briefly touched on the subject of software for giving us access to the market. In the following section we shall consider in more detail the types of applications available for working in the financial markets.

We Need Specialized Software to Access the Market

As you will realize, we need specialized software, but what do we actually require and what would be best?

Types of software for working in financial markets

Brokerages with on-line market access and other services offer different types of programs free of charge.

Some companies offer purely trading platforms without any market analysis functions.

Others offer both trading platforms and market analysis software. These usually consist of separate applications, which is a little inconvenient because you have to launch one program for trading and the other for analysis.

There are even brokerages which only provide a trading platform and advise clients to purchase additional software for market analysis & forecasting. As a general rule, stand-alone software is rather expensive and may require a one-time payment, a monthly/annual charge or both.

Therefore, the best choice is a stand-alone application that integrates both market analysis and the ability to execute trades.

Our software of choice is MetaTrader 4. This trade terminal allows you to analyze markets and, at the same time, execute trades directly from the charts.

We discuss MetaTrader 4 in more detail later in this book.

Types of Orders

There are many different types of orders, some of which are specific to stock trading. Fortunately, it is not necessary for us to learn all of them.

In our opinion, it is more than adequate to examine just those order types used in MetaTrader 4 – this will encompass the types of orders which are most commonly used in the FOREX market.

Client terminals allow the preparation of requests to the broker for execution of trading operations. Moreover, a terminal allows control and management of open positions. To achieve this, several types of trading orders are used.

An order is a client's commitment to a brokerage company to perform a trade operation.

The types of orders we will be using are:

Market Order

A Market Order is a commitment to the brokerage company to buy or sell a security at the current price. Execution of this order results in opening of a trade position.

Securities are bought at the ASK price and sold at the BID price.

Stop Loss and Take Profit orders (described below) can be attached to a market order if your broker offers "instant execution" but most "ECN" brokers (who **do not** trade against you) will not.

The **Execution mode** of market orders depends on the type of security traded.

Pending Order

Pending order is the client's commitment to the brokerage company to buy or sell a security at a pre-defined price in the future. This type of orders is used for the opening of a trade position provided the future price quotes reach the pre-defined level.

There are four types of pending orders available on the terminal:

> **Buy Limit** — Buy provided the future "ASK" price is equal to the pre-defined value. The current price level is higher than the value of the placed order.
>
> Orders of this type are usually placed in anticipation that the security price, having fallen to a certain level, will increase.
>
> **Buy Stop** — Buy provided the future "ASK" price is equal to the pre-defined value. The current price level is lower than the value of the placed order.
>
> Orders of this type are usually placed in anticipation that the security price, having reached a certain level, will continue to increase.
>
> **Sell Limit** — Sell provided the future "BID" price is equal to the pre-defined value. The current price level is lower than the value of the placed order.
>
> Orders of this type are usually placed in anticipation of that the security price, having increased to a certain level, will fall.
>
> **Sell Stop** — Sell provided the future "BID" price is equal to the pre-defined value. The current price level is higher than the value of the placed order.
>
> Orders of this type are usually placed in anticipation of that the security price, having reached a certain level, will continue to fall.

Stop Loss and/or *Take Profit* orders can be specified with a pending order regardless of broker type. After a pending order has triggered, its Stop Loss and/or Take Profit levels will be attached to the newly opened position automatically.

Stop Loss

A Stop Loss order is used to minimize losses if the security price has started to move in an unprofitable direction. If the security price reaches this level, the position will be closed automatically.

Such orders are always connected to an open position or a pending order.

The brokerage company can place them together only with a market or a pending order. The terminal compares long positions against the ASK price and short positions against the BID price.

There is also an automated Stop Loss order called a **Trailing Stop** which continuously adjusts its position to a fixed distance from the current price while a trade is increasing in profit but holds its position if the current price starts to move against the trade, thus locking in profits.

Take Profit

The Take Profit order is intended for automatically exiting with a profit when the security price has reached a certain level. Execution of this order results in closing of the position.

It is always connected to an open position or a pending order.

The order can be requested together only with a market or a pending order. The terminal compares long positions against the ASK price and short positions against the BID price.

Important Note:

Execution prices for all trade operations are defined by the broker;

Stop Loss and Take Profit orders will only be executed for an open position, not for pending orders as the main order to which the Stop Loss / Take Profit relates has not yet triggered.

Speed of Order Execution

Speed of execution for an order is a very important aspect of any on-line trade operation.

Whilst speed is naturally important for managers of large funds and for traders who trade on a long-term basis, it is **extremely** important to us – traders whose profit depends on seconds or even fractions of a second.

Not long ago, orders could only be conducted by telephone.

Today, some brokerage companies still insist that trades above a certain size, e.g. $1,000,000 for single trading position, are placed by telephone.

Nowadays, most companies have switched to so-called "instant execution" or "market execution" of orders. This means that the time taken for the operation (the period between when you issue an order to the broker to open or close a trade position and the actual opening or closing of the trade) is typically 1-5 seconds, though this time period depends very much on the quality of your Internet connection and the liquidity available to the broker.

So, we have looked at almost all aspects required for trading and now we need to move on to learn about forecasting market behavior.

Why forecast? Well, you certainly would not drive your car while blindfolded so why would you think about trading that way?

Let us look at these common tools which help us to trade more efficiently.

CHAPTER 6
HOW TO FORECAST
MARKET BEHAVIOR

Can we forecast the future?

Why yes, of course! Any financial market can be analyzed and forecast in some way.

Through the medium of specialized sciences we call technical and fundamental analysis we can assess the probabilities of a market's direction in the future.

Fundamental Analysis

Fundamental analysis is an analysis of a country's national qualities (macroeconomics). Fundamental analysis is more pivotal in its power to move the markets with the whims of its daily, weekly, monthly, etc. economical news releases.

Any kind of breaking news, such as some unexpected event of national importance, can break any market prediction that is based on technical analysis alone. We will discuss technical analysis much more in the next section.

The most important macroeconomic indicators are:

1. Factors influencing the market include: Consumer Price Index (CPI), Orders for durable goods, Employment data, Gross National Product (GNP), new house construction, international trade balances, personal income and outlay, Producer Price Index, retail sales, etc.

2. Other important indicators: Beige book, Consumer confidence, Current account, session of the Federal Open Market Committee (FOMC Meeting), Leading Indicators, initial requirements of unemployment benefits (Jobless claims)

3. Reports of heads of the governments, heads of the central banks, outstanding economists concerning a situation in the market

4. Changing monetary and credit policy

5. Sessions of the big seven - the trading and economic unions

There is no real need to worry about "surprise" results. These macroeconomic indicator reports are published at known times of the year and rarely contain unexpected results.

Let us now look at a typical example for one trading day which is shown in the following table:

This table shows a typical example for one day:

Wednesday, 19 April 2006

Time GMT	Country	Period	Macroeconomic indicators	Prior	Forecast	Actual
06:00	Germany	Mar	PPI	0.7% m/m 5.9% y/y	0.3% m/m 5.6% y/y	
08:00	Norway	Mar	Trade Balance	+nok29.2B		
08:30	Great Britain	Apr	BOE publishes minutes of April 5-6 MPC meeting			
11:00	USA	Apr 14	MBA Mortgage Application Index	-5.5% to 579.4		
12:30	USA	Mar	CPI ex food & energy	+0.1%	+0.2%	
12:30	USA	Mar	Consumer Price Index	+0.1%	+0.4%	
12:30	Canada	Feb	Wholesale inventories	+1.4%		
12:30	Canada	Feb	Wholesale sales	+1.8%		
12:30	Canada	Mar	Leading indicator	+0.2%		
12:30	Canada	Feb	Intl sec transaction	+C$3.0 bn		
13:00	USA		International Monetary Fund to release semi-annual World Economic Outlook ahead of annual spring meetings, in Washington.			
14:30	USA	Apr 14	EIA Crude Oil Stocks	+3.2 mn to 346.0 mn brls		
18:30	USA		Treasury Secretary John Snow to address the World Health Care Congress, in Washington.			
23:50	Japan	Mar	Trade Balance	Y955.7B	Y704.8B	

As you can see, the right hand part of the table consists of three columns: *Prior*, *Forecast* and *Actual*.

"*Prior*" means that a previously defined index had some value in the past for a defined period of time (week, month, quarter).

"*Forecast*" means economists and professional traders, based on specific calculations, are waiting for this index value for the week, month or quarter.

"*Actual*" means the real value of the index is unknown (or, at least, unpublished) so far.

Of course, if you are a beginner, then these aspects can be difficult to understand.

Do not worry! Help is at hand.

Most brokerages offer a service providing this information to their clients free of charge.

Common detailed Fundamental Analysis for an index:

Fundamental Analysis: ISM services index

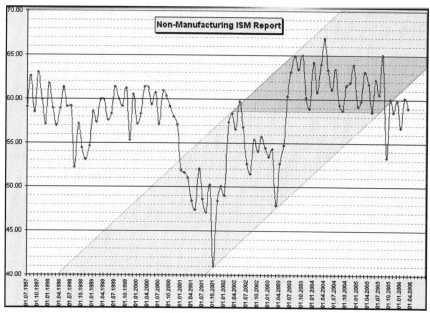

The last indicator value

Analysis: This index was in an uptrend from the end of 2001. During 2002 it stayed above 50, signifying that the service sector was increasing.

From the middle of 2003 this index stabilized within the indicated range. Its decrease in September was triggered by the hurricane and, though it recovered in October, it is still quite low.

Conclusion:
This index signifies some weakness in the mid-term perspective. ISM services index for March may be more positive than forecast.

2nd example of Fundamental Analysis for a day:

Wednesday, 5 April 2006

Time Zone (GMT)	Country	Period	Indicator	Forecast	Prior	Level of importance
01:30	Australia		RBA Board Meeting Outcome	5.50%	5.50%	3

Note: Most likely, the interest rate remains constant.	Possible influence on an exchange rate		
	Forecast	Above forecast	Below forecast
	AUD →	AUD ↑↑	AUD ↓↓

Time Zone (GMT)	Country	Period	Indicator	Forecast	Prior	Level of importance
09:30	Great Britain	February	Industrial Production	0.2% м/м, -0.9% y/y	0.4% м/м, -1.3% y/y	2

Note: Decrease in a level of production will put pressure upon a rate of sterling.	Possible influence on an exchange rate		
	Forecast	Above forecast	Below forecast
	GBP →	GBP ???	GBP ↓

Time Zone (GMT)	Country	Period	Indicator	Forecast	Prior	Level of importance
14:30	USA		Statement of chairman of Federal Reserve Ben Bernanke in Washington.			3

Note: Swings are possible in the market. I recommend operating extremely cautiously with the dollar at this time.	Possible influence on an exchange rate		
	Forecast	Above forecast	Below forecast
	USD ???	USD ???	USD ???

Time Zone (GMT)	Country	Period	Indicator	Forecast	Prior	Level of importance
15:00	USA		Statement of Minister of Finance John Snow on questions of the budget for 2007 in Washington.			3

Note: At this time I do not recommend entering USD transactions.	Possible influence on an exchange rate		
	Forecast	Above forecast	Below forecast
	USD ???	USD ???	USD ???

See Notes on the following page

Notes:

Above the forecast – *the actual value is mathematically larger than the forecast value (for example, 5% > 4.3% and -49 > -51).*

Below the forecast – *the actual value is mathematically smaller than the forecast value (for example, 4.1% < 4.3% and -61 < -51).*

Fundamental analysis does not provide absolute indication in market analysis and will always consist of a complex of possible tendencies.

The level of importance of each economic indicator can be deduced by studying the influence that indicator exerted on an exchange rate over a period of several years.

The level of importance of a given indicator can be over or underestimated depending on the market conditions at the time and the degree of expectancy by a market of the announced result.

Explanation of the elements of the forecast:

Importance of the Economic Data

1   The announcement of a given result is not expected to influence a currency and, most likely, its publication will be little more than a statistical fact

2   The announcement of a given result is expected to influence a currency for the current session at most

3   The announcement of a given result is expected to influence a currency for a day, a week or even a month

Possible Influence on an Exchange Rate

→   The output of the economic indicator (presumably) does not render action on an exchange rate

↑   The output of the economic indicator will (presumably) cause growth of an exchange rate

↓   The output of the economic indicator will (presumably) cause a decline of an exchange rate

↓↓   The output of the economic indicator will (presumably) cause strong (very strong) decline of an exchange rate

↑↑   The output of the economic indicator will (presumably) cause strong (very strong) growth of an exchange rate

?   It is very difficult to predict movement of the currency after the publication of the data (more often it happens before publication of carryovers from sessions of central banks, statements of large political figures, publications of economic reports (the Beige book (USA), Tankan (Japan), etc.)

As you can see, brokerages will try their best to help you with all kinds of trading information. In time, you will be able to understand everything very clearly.

Now, let us move on to Technical Analysis. This will only be a brief introduction as there are a lot of books available on this topic. We will cover what is required to successfully use this trading system.

Technical analysis

Technical analysis is research of market dynamics done mainly with the help of charts, and for the purpose of forecasting future price movement.

Technical analysis comprises several approaches to the study of price movement which are interconnected within the framework of one harmonious theory.

This type of analysis studies the price movement in the market by analyzing three market factors: price, volume, and in the case of futures contracts, the number of open positions.

Of these three factors, the primary one for technical analysis is that of price. Changes in other factors are studied, mainly in order to confirm the correctness of the identified price trend. This technical theory, just like any theory, has its core postulates.

Technical analysts base their research on three axioms:

Market movement considers everything

This is the most important postulate of technical analysis and is crucial to understand in order to grasp the procedures of analysis.

Put simply, any factor that influences the price of securities, whether economic, political, or psychological, has already been taken into account and reflected in the price chart.

In other words, every price change is accompanied by a change in external factors. The main inference of this premise is the necessity to follow closely the price movements and analyze them.

By means of analyzing price charts and multiple other indicators, a technical analyst reaches the point that the market, itself, shows him/her the trend it will most likely follow.

This premise is in conflict with fundamental analysis where the attention is primarily paid to the study of factors, after analysis of which, conclusions as to the market trends are made.

Thus, if the demand is higher than the supply, a fundamental analyst will come to the conclusion that the price will increase. A technical analyst, by contrast, makes his/her conclusions in the opposite order: since price has increased, demand must be higher than supply.

Prices move with the trend

This assumption is the basis for all methods of technical analysis, as a market that moves in accordance with trends can be analyzed, unlike a chaotic market. This postulate that the price movement is a result of a trend has two effects:

One implies that the current trend is likely to continue and will not reverse, thus excluding disorderly chaotic market movement.

The second implies that the current trend will continue until the opposite trend sets in.

History repeats itself

Technical analysis and study of market dynamics are closely related to the study of human psychology so the graphical price models identified and classified over the last hundred years depict core characteristics of the psychological state of the market.

Primarily, they show the moods currently prevailing in the market, whether bullish or bearish. Since these models worked in the past, we have reason to suppose that they will work in the future, for they are based on human psychology which remains almost unchanged over the years.

With the above in mind, we can reword the last postulate - history repeats itself - in a slightly different way:

The key to understanding the future lies in the study of the past

Complex Trading Systems

Trading Systems created by advanced traders

As a rule, "beginner" traders search for literature devoted to trading financial markets. They study market basics and as they begin to understand how they function, they study the technical and fundamental analysis.

While continuing with their studies, they open a virtual trading account and start to practice their theoretical knowledge.

Of course, it takes time.

Once they start to earn "income" using virtual money, they open the real trading account, fund it with real money and start trading with the intention of receiving a real money profit.

A trader looks at various indicators, trying to define which are best suited to their style of trading. In parallel, a trader can use the free and paid services giving trading recommendations.

In due course, step by step, a trader begins to form their own approach to trading based on certain rules for using those particular indicators or other trading tools (a set of carefully chosen indicators, with certain parameters, for example).

Eventually, the trader forms their own unique approach to trading; their trading strategy or trading system.

Put simply, a system consists of identifying a set of events or situations which arise in the market and confirming these as good (or bad) by comparing them with a known set of parameters and technical indicators. When all or most of these events occur at any one time, it is a signal to buy (or sell).

It is important for the systems developed by a trader to be computerized at the earliest opportunity. This will allow their automatic execution without the trader having to be directly involved.

Many trading platforms such as MT4 allow the user to program algorithms (a procedure or formula for solving a problem, created in the form of a script that is run on your computer) and build them into a trading system. This makes it possible for trade positions to be opened and closed automatically when certain conditions occur.

The basic advantages of this approach are:

1. There is no human factor, i.e. a trader, as a person, will be free from excessive emotions. Nerves are kept (relatively) intact!

2. The trader will have more free time. Traders should not be constantly "chained" to the computer screen.

The basic disadvantages of this approach:

1. As all these systems are executed by the client's computer (within the trading terminal or platform), instead of on the brokerage's server, it can create a different sort of force majeure situation such as: problems with your PC (computer lock-ups, etc.), power failures or internet connection problems.

2. There is more chance of missing unexpected fundamental news.

The given approach has advantages and also disadvantages – ultimately it is up to you.

As for ourselves, we use our own trading system: "**MAIN FOREX SYSTEM**" which is semi-mechanical and discussed in the next section.

Trading Systems offered by financial companies

As has been mentioned before, there are many companies offering "ready for trading" trade recommendations or instant trade alerts (for intraday trading). Charges for these facilities can be monthly, quarterly or annual. These services can be in the form of "ready for use" software, e-mail mail alerts or notifications via instant messenger services.

The cost for such services can be quite high: around $200 per month (or more) for trading alerts.

Software can be even more expensive. We know of companies offering software for generating trading signals/alerts that costs over $9,000!

In fairness, these services can be extremely useful for people who are very busy and simply unable to watch the markets all of the time.

In our case, we prefer to use our own trading system and are confident that you will like using it too.

In the next section we will look at the technical tools used in our system – The **MAIN FOREX SYSTEM**.

CHAPTER 7
MAIN FOREX SYSTEM

Description of the system

The **MAIN FOREX SYSTEM** consists of two approaches: A Day-Trading system with the option of keeping positions overnight (short-term system) and a Scalping system. Part II of the book covers advanced strategies, break-out system and other interesting aspects of FX trading.

Depending on market conditions, exiting trades can be maintained until the next day, or even for several days. It really depends on your risk appetite and temperament – trading can be stressful!

Important:

Every knowledgeable trader knows that day-trading (intraday trading) means opening and closing your positions within a single trading day.

*In other words, you should not leave positions open overnight; but in this system you **may** leave your positions open overnight (or even for several days) if market conditions are good.*

*For example, after opening a position, you might find yourself in a strong up or down trend movement that has developed. In these circumstances you can use a **trailing stop** to determine your exit.*

This system can be used no matter which direction the markets are headed - up or down.

So, if the market is going up, **we trade it upwards**.

If the market is going down, we also **trade it – downwards!**

There are several strategies for entering a market and several for exiting. Later in this book, we also discuss something called **trailing stops**.

The purpose of using this system

Is it possible to turn $1,000 into $1,000,000 in 24 months by trading FOREX?

Did you notice that we added "$" to the figures? Make no mistake. We are talking about making **real money.**

Right now, it may seem like a dream or some cheap advertising trick... but it absolutely is not. It is real and **it is achievable!**

Here is something for you to think about:

Larry Williams, a well-known trader, entered a futures trading contest for international traders and grew a $10,000 account into over $1,000,000 in just 12 months... then repeated that feat the following year! Some time later, his daughter followed in her father's footsteps and did the same.

They traded futures but we have the FOREX market with much greater profit potential than other financial markets.

So, let us see how much we can earn on the way to reaching our goal and thus achieving our purpose.

It your original $1,000 deposit grew by **as little as 2.5% per day** from risking 10% of it per trade (in this instance, 25-31 pips with leverage of 1:100) then at the end of a 24 month continuous trading period **your account balance would be $263,819,900!!**

> **Note**: In this example it is assumed that you:
>
> **a)** used correct 0.1 lot trade increments as your account balance permitted and,
> **b)** did not make a withdrawal of funds from your account, otherwise the result would be quite different.

So, how is such a great sum created?

The secret is a combination of compounding plus the use of special money management rules.

There are basically 22 trading days and 8 non-trading days in each calendar month.

For currency pairs with a fixed pip value of $10 (EUR/USD for example), **2.5% per day offers between 42% and 72% potential compounded growth per month.**

Let us assume that you opened your live trading account with a $1,000 deposit on 1st of January 2012 and traded until 1st of January 2014.

The following tables show how your investment increases month by month.

1st 12 Months		2nd 12 Months	
End of Month	Balance	End of Month	Balance
January	$1,550	January	$670,550
February	$2,200	February	$1,154,075
March	$3,450	March	$1,986,475
April	$5,550	April	$3,419,525
May	$9,150	May	$5,886,650
June	$15,450	June	$10,133,900
July	$26,275	July	$17,445,875
August	$44,825	August	$30,034,000
September	$76,800	September	$51,705,375
October	$131,800	October	$89,014,150
November	$226,575	November	$153,243,900
December	$389,700	December	$263,819,900

Note: *Amounts shown have been rounded down.*

Now, imagine if you had started with a $10,000 deposit!

General Money Management Rules for the Main FOREX System

Important:

*The Money Management Rules explained below apply **only** to the **Main FOREX System**. Use of these rules with other trading systems could result in unexpected losses.*

You should already know what **Money Management Rules** are for and also that such rules are different for each trader. If not, you should understand that their main purpose is to prevent you from using (or losing!) all of your capital at once.

For us, an acceptable level of risk is between 8% and 10% of our account balance on any single trade but you must decide what is comfortable for you. Trading with a fixed number of lots is one thing, but using different levels of stop orders is quite another situation. Let us clarify this.

> *Note: We will be trading the EUR/USD, USD/CHF and USD/JPY currency pairs.*

For example, if you open a 0.1 lot position with a deposit of $1,000 and a stop order at 100 pips (EUR/USD - fixed value for pips) you are risking 10% of your account, as the pip value of a full (1.0) EUR/USD lot is $10.00. For USD/CHF and USD/JPY currency pairs we have:

USD/CHF (floating pip value), about $8, risk – 8%

USD/JPY (floating pip value), about $9, risk – 9%

Our strategy recommends a stop order distance of 45 pips but, as you will notice, for our $1,000 example account, that gives differing risks depending upon the currency traded:

EUR/USD - 4.5% for one 0.1 lot position

USD/CHF - 3.6% for one 0.1 lot position

USD/JPY – 4.05% for one 0.1 lot position

As we mentioned before, all the calculations of percentages were related to a pair with a fixed pip value ($10), in which case we needed to earn 25 pips per day.

This means that the number of pips we need to earn each day for pairs with floating pip values will be different:

USD/CHF - $8 pip value - requires 31 pips per day

USD/JPY - $9 pip value - requires 28 pips per day

Lot management for medium risk & aggressive traders:

We open a position of twice the lot size determined by the Money Management rules – using MetaTrader, this is best achieved by placing two individual orders i.e. for a $1,000 account, two orders of 0.1 lots rather than one single order of 0.2 lots.

The initial Stop Loss level is 45 pips from the entry point.

> **Note:** Technical exit strategies will be covered later in chapter 10 - "Trading rules for the Main FOREX System".

The risk for various currency pairs:

EUR/USD - 9%

USD/CHF - 7.2%

USD/JPY – 8.1%

As you can see, all risks are acceptable (to us, at least) and, hopefully, now you will understand the purpose of using two orders.

Once the currency pair has moved a set number of pips in our direction (the number of pips varies between currency pairs), we close one order and set the Stop Loss level on the remaining order to the entry point (break-even) level.

Examples of multiple exit points for different pairs

The following examples are based on a $10,000 trading account and 1.0-lot orders have been used in the profit calculations.

To obtain the "per trade" profit for a mini account (i.e. an account trading 0.1 lots), simply divide the profit figure by 10.

If you have a micro account (i.e. an account trading 0.01 lots), divide the profit figure by 100.

USD/CHF

Open two 1.0 lot orders. Upon reaching 31 pips profit, we close one order and move the stop loss level of the remaining order to our entry (break-even) point.

Illustration of the USD/CHF trade

$1,018 profit in two hours

We entered with a buy order at a price of 1.2929 (the low of the price bar was actually 1.2919) and the stop loss level set at 1.2884.

Price reached 1.2965 which, after deducting the 5 pip spread, gave us our 31 pip profit at our target exit price of 1.2960.

Having closed one order and moved the stop loss level of the remaining order to its break-even / entry point (1.2929), we have already achieved our goal for the day by earning $250 (2.5%) and now we have nothing to lose but the unrealized gains from our second order.

So, what now?

At this point, we have a banked profit of $250 from the first order and the market price has now peaked at 1.3037.

Using exit strategy №1 (more about this later), we close the remaining lot at a price of 1.3025.

That second order earned us 96 pips or $768.

The result: in just 2 hours we earned $1,018 which is **4 times more than the plan.**

EUR/USD

Open two 1.0 lot orders. Upon reaching 25 pips profit, we close one order and move the stop loss level of the remaining order to our entry (break-even) point.

Illustration of the EUR/USD trade

$1,150 profit in two hours

We entered with a sell order at a price of 1.2025 (the high of the price bar was actually 1.2031) and the stop loss level set at 1.2070.

Price reached 1.1997 which, after deducting the 3 pip spread, gave us our 25 pip profit at our target exit price of 1.2000

Having closed one order and moved the stop loss level for the remaining order to its break-even / entry point (1.2025), we have once again achieved our goal for the day by earning $250 (2.5%) and, as before, we now have nothing to lose but the unrealized gains from our second order.

So, what happened next?

Well, we already had our $248 banked profit from the first order and floating profits of $248 from the second order when price actually fell to 1.1930.

Using exit strategy №1 (more about this later), we closed the remaining order at a price of 1.1935 which gave us a profit of 90 pips or $900.

The result: for about 2 hours "work", we earned $1,150 – almost **5 times more** than the plan.

Okay – you will probably be getting a little bored with these examples so just one more…

USD/JPY

Open two 1.0-lot orders. Upon reaching 28 pips profit, we close one order and move the stop loss level of the remaining order to our entry (break-even) point.

Illustration of the USD/JPY trade

$610 profit in six hours

We entered with a buy order at a price of 113.20 (the low of the price bar was actually 113.13) and the stop loss level set at 112.75.

Price reached 113.51 which, after deducting the 3 pip spread, gave us our 28 pip profit and target exit price of 113.48

Having closed one order and moved the stop loss level for the remaining order to its break-even / entry point (113.20), we have achieved our goal for the day by earning $250 (2.5%) and now, just as before, we have nothing to lose but our unrealized gains from our second order.

As expected, we have our banked profit of $252 from the first lot and the market price kindly continued up to 113.68.

Following the rules of exit strategy №1 (more about this later), we closed the second order at a price of 113.60 which gave us a profit of 40 pips or $360.

The result: after a grueling 6 hours we earned $610 - about 2.5 times more then the plan.

We have looked at the Money Management Rules for the **Main FOREX System**. Now we need to know about the "tools" used for making trades.

What Tools Are Used In This System?

We are going to use the following standard indicators:

* Trend lines of support and resistance
* Exponential Moving Averages
* Stochastic Oscillator
* MACD
* RSI
* Williams' Percentage Range

These are the only tools we need to make this work. Nothing more. NO difficult (exotic) indicators or intricate calculations.

Description of Technical Indicators used in the System

Here we are going to describe the technical indicators used in the system.

Support and Resistance

Think of prices for financial instruments as a result of a head-to-head battle between a bull (the buyer) and a bear (the seller).

Bulls push prices higher, and bears lower them. The direction that prices actually move shows who is winning the battle.

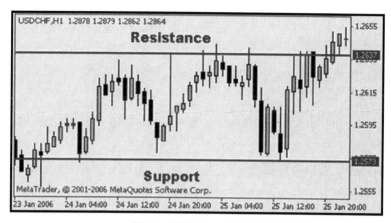

Flat or Sideways Trend

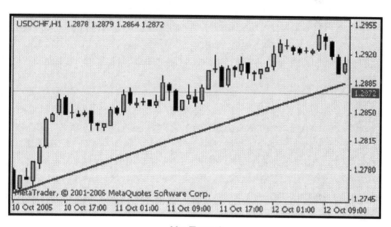

Up Trend

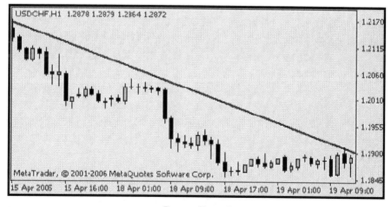

Down Trend

Support is a level at which bulls (i.e. buyers) take control over price and prevent it from falling lower.

Resistance, on the other hand, is the point at which sellers (bears) take control of prices and prevent them from rising higher. The price at which a trade takes place is the price at which a bulls and bears agree to do business. It represents the consensus of their expectations.

Support levels indicate the price where the majority of investors believe that prices will move higher.

Resistance levels indicate the price at which the majority of investors feel prices will move lower.

Investor expectations, however, change with time, and they often do so abruptly. The development of support and resistance levels is probably the most noticeable and re-occurring event on price charts.

The breaking-through of support/resistance levels can be triggered by fundamental changes that are above or below an investor's expectations (e.g. changes in earnings, management, competition, etc.) or by self-fulfilling prophecy (investors buy as they "see" prices rise). The cause is not as significant as the effect: new expectations lead to new price levels. There are also support/resistance levels which are more emotional.

Supply and demand

There is nothing mysterious about support and resistance: it is classic supply and demand. Remembering your "Economics 101" class, supply-demand lines show what the supply and demand will be at a given price.

The supply line shows the quantity (i.e. the number of shares) that sellers are willing to supply at a given price. When prices increase, the quantity of sellers also increases as more investors are willing to sell at these higher prices.

The demand line shows the number of shares that buyers are willing to buy at a given price. When prices increase, they decrease the quantity of investors that are willing to buy at the higher prices.

At any given price, a supply/demand chart shows how many buyers and sellers are in a market. In a free market, these lines are continually changing. Investors' expectations change, and so do the prices buyers and sellers feel are acceptable.

A breakout above a resistance level is evidence of an upward shift in the demand line as more buyers become willing to buy at higher prices. Similarly, the failure of a support level shows that the supply line has shifted downward.

The foundation of most technical analysis tools is rooted in the concept of supply and demand. Charts of prices for financial instruments give us a superb view of these forces in action.

Traders' remorse

After a support/resistance level has been broken through, it is common for traders to ask themselves to what extent new prices represent the facts.

For example, after a breakout above a resistance level, buyers and sellers may both question the validity of the new price and may decide to sell. This creates a phenomenon that is referred to as "traders' remorse": prices return to a support/resistance level following a price breakout.

The effect on prices following this remorseful period is crucial. One of two things can happen: either the consensus of expectations will be that the new price is not warranted, in which case prices will move back to their previous level; or investors will accept the new price, in which case prices will continue to move in the direction of the break-through.

In some cases, immediately following traders' remorse, the consensus of expectations is that a new higher price is not warranted, a classic "bull trap" (or false breakout) is created. For example, price broke through a certain resistance level (luring in a herd of bulls who expected prices to move higher), and then prices dropped back to below the resistance level leaving the bulls holding overpriced stock.

Similar sentiment creates a "bear trap". Prices drop below a support level long enough to get the bears to sell (or sell short) and then bounce back above the support level leaving the bears out of the market.

The other thing that can happen following traders' remorse is that investors' expectations may change causing the new price to be accepted. In this case, prices will continue to move in the direction of the penetration.

A good way to quantify expectations following a breakout is with the volume associated with the price breakout. If prices break through the support/resistance level with a large increase in volume and the traders' remorse period is on relatively low volume, it implies that the new expectations will rule (a minority of investors are remorseful).

Conversely, if the breakout is on moderate volume and the "remorseful" period is on increased volume, it implies that very few investor expectations have changed and a return to the original expectations (i.e. original prices) is warranted.

Resistance becomes support

When a resistance level is successfully broken through by a price, this level becomes a support level. Similarly, when a support level is successfully broken through by a price, this level becomes a resistance level.

The reason for this is that a new "generation" of bulls appears who refused to buy when prices were low. Now they are anxious to buy at any time price returns to the previous level.

Similarly, when prices drop below a support level, that level often becomes a resistance level that prices have a difficult time breaking through.

When prices approach the previous support level, investors seek to limit their losses by selling.

Moving Averages (MAs)

In order to understand what an EMA is, we first need to know about a simple moving average (MA).

The Moving Average Technical Indicator shows the mean instrument price value for a certain period of time. When one calculates the moving average, one "averages out" the instrument price for this time period. As the price changes, its moving average either increases, or decreases.

There are four different types of moving averages: Simple (also referred to as Arithmetic), Exponential, Smoothed and Linear Weighted. Moving averages may be calculated for any sequential data set, including opening and closing prices, highest and lowest prices, trading volume or any other indicators. It is often the case when double moving averages are used.

The only reason why moving averages of different types diverge considerably from each other is if its weight coefficients, which are assigned to the latest data, are different. In this example we are talking about a simple moving average, all prices for the time period in question are equal in value. Exponential and Linear Weighted Moving Averages attach more value to the latest prices.

The most common way to interpret the price moving average is to compare its dynamics to the price action. When the instrument price rises above its moving average, a buy signal appears. If price falls below its moving average, what we have is a sell signal.

This trading system, which is based on the moving average, is not designed to provide entries into the market right at its lowest points, and exits right on the peaks. It allows traders to act according to the following trend: to buy soon after price reaches the bottom and to sell soon after price has reached its peak.

Moving averages may also be applied to indicators. This is where the interpretation of indicator moving averages is similar to the interpretation of price moving averages: if the indicator rises above its moving average, it indicates that the ascending indicator movement is likely to continue: if the indicator falls below its moving average, it indicates that it is likely to continue going downward.

Exponential Moving Average (EMA)

An exponentially smoothed moving average is calculated by adding the moving average of a certain share of the current closing price to the previous value. With exponentially smoothed moving averages, the latest prices are of more value.

For our trading system we will be using a 5 period EMA of both the Lows and Highs of the price bars as support and resistance levels.

Important: Where charts are shown in grayscale, be aware that the 5EMA of the Highs is shown lighter than the 5EMA of the Lows and runs near the Highs of each price bar of the chart. The opposite is true for 5EMA of the Lows. The 20EMA of the Closes is shown in black and should be easy to identify. The example chart below shows the 5EMAs of the Highs and Lows:

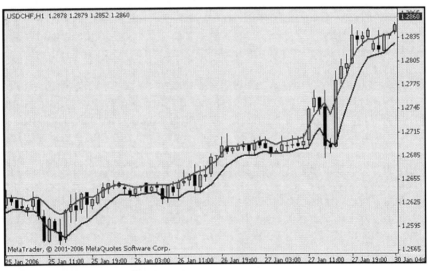

Two 5 Period EMAs: one of the Highs and one of the Lows

Charts showing the 20EMA of the Closes will appear later in this book.

Stochastic Oscillator

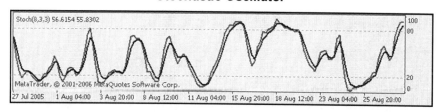

The Stochastic Oscillator Technical Indicator compares where a security's price closed relative to its price range over a given time period.

The Stochastic Oscillator is displayed as two lines. The main line is called %K. The second line, called %D, is a Moving Average of %K.

The %K line is usually displayed as a solid line and the %D line is usually displayed as a dotted line.

There are several ways to interpret a Stochastic Oscillator.

Three popular methods include:

- Buy when the Oscillator (either %K or %D) falls below a specific level (e.g. 20) and then rises above that level. Sell when the Oscillator rises above a specific level (e.g. 80) and then falls below that level;

- Buy when the %K line rises above the %D line and sell when the %K line falls below the %D line;

- Identifying divergences. For instance: where prices are making a series of new highs and the Stochastic Oscillator is failing to surpass its previous highs.

We will be using the Stochastic Oscillator for:

- finding divergence with the price of a currency pair

- indicating an alert for opening a trade position

(MACD) Moving Average Convergence/Divergence

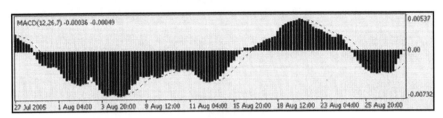

MACD

The MACD proves most effective in wide-swinging trading markets.

There are three popular ways to use the Moving Average Convergence / Divergence: crossovers, overbought/oversold conditions and divergences.

Crossovers

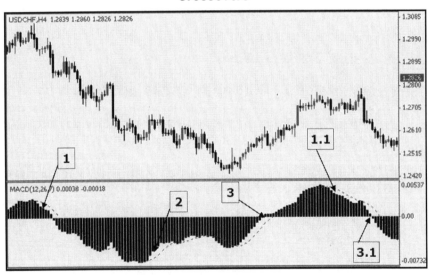

The basic MACD trading rule is to sell when the MACD falls below **[markers 1, 1.1]** its signal line. Similarly, a buy signal occurs when the Moving Average Convergence/Divergence rises above its signal line **[marker 2]**. It is also popular to buy/sell when the MACD goes above/below zero **[markers 3, 3.1]**.

Overbought/oversold conditions

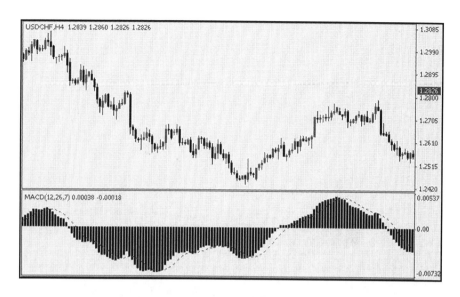

The MACD is also useful as an overbought/oversold indicator.

When the shorter moving average pulls away dramatically from the longer moving average (i.e. the MACD rises), it is likely that the security price is overextending and will soon return to more realistic levels.

Divergence

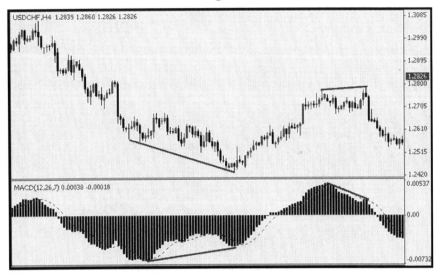

An indication that an end to the current trend may be near occurs when the MACD diverges from the security.

A bullish divergence occurs when the Moving Average Convergence / Divergence indicator is making new highs while prices fail to reach new highs.

A bearish divergence occurs when the MACD is making new lows while prices fail to reach new lows.

Both of these divergences are most significant when they occur at relatively overbought/oversold levels.

We will be using the MACD for:

- finding divergence with the price of a currency pair

- indicating an alert for opening a trade position

(RSI) Relative Strength Index Technical Indicator

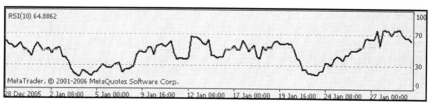

Relative Strength Index

The Relative Strength Index Technical Indicator (RSI) is a price-following oscillator that ranges between 0 and 100.

When Wilder introduced the Relative Strength Index, he recommended using a 14-day RSI.

Since then, the 9-day and 25-day Relative Strength Index indicators have also gained popularity.

A popular method of analyzing the RSI is to look for a divergence in which the security is making a new high, but the RSI is failing to surpass its previous high. This divergence is an indication of an impending reversal.

When the Relative Strength Index then turns down and falls below its most recent trough, it is said to have completed a "failure swing". The failure swing is considered a confirmation of the impending reversal.

Ways to use Relative Strength Index for chart analysis:

Tops and bottoms The Relative Strength Index usually tops out above 70 and bottoms out below 30. It normally forms these tops and bottoms before the underlying price chart;

Chart Formations The RSI often forms chart patterns such as head and shoulders or triangles that may or may not be visible on the price chart;

Failure swing (Support or Resistance penetrations or breakouts) This is where the Relative Strength Index surpasses a previous high (peak) or falls below a recent low (trough);

Support and Resistance Levels The Relative Strength Index shows, sometimes more clearly than prices themselves, levels of support and resistance.

Divergences As discussed above, divergences occur when price makes a new high (or low) that is not confirmed by a new high (or low) in the Relative Strength Index. Prices usually correct and move in the direction of the RSI.

We will be using Relative Strength Index as a secondary confirmative indicator for entries and exits of trades.

Williams' Percent Range Technical Indicator (%R)

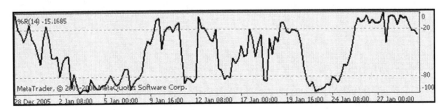

Williams' Percent Range

Williams' Percent Range Technical Indicator (%R) is a dynamic technical indicator which determines whether the market is overbought or oversold.

Williams' %R is very similar to the Stochastic Oscillator. The only real differences are that %R has an upside down scale and the Stochastic Oscillator has internal smoothing.

To show the indicator in this upside down fashion, you need to place a minus symbol before the Williams Percent Range values (e.g. -30%).

Indicator values ranging between -80 and -100% indicate that the market is oversold. Indicator values ranging between 0 and -20% indicate that the market is overbought.

As with all overbought/oversold indicators, it is best to wait for the security's price to change direction before placing your trades. For example, if an overbought/oversold indicator is showing an overbought condition, it is wise to wait for the security's price to turn down before selling the security.

An interesting phenomenon of the Williams Percent Range indicator is its uncanny ability to anticipate a reversal in the underlying security's price. The indicator almost always forms a peak and turns down a few days before the security's price peaks and turns down.

Likewise, Williams Percent Range usually creates a trough and turns up a few days before the security's price turns up.

We will be using Williams' Percent Range as an overbought/oversold indicator which will be confirming the overbought/oversold condition of the corresponding currency.

Summary of indicators and their settings:

1-Hour Chart
- 5 period EMA of the Highs
- 5 period EMA of the Lows
- 20 period EMA of the Closes
- Stochastic (5,3,3)
- MACD (12,26,9)

15-Minute Chart
- 20 period EMA of the Closes
- Stochastic (5,3,3)
- Williams %R (14)
- RSI (10)

CHAPTER 8
BROKERAGE AND TRADE
TERMINAL

Of course, in order to trade FOREX we need a good brokerage and a good Trade Terminal (Workstation).

Recommended Brokerage

To access the FOREX market, a trader requires an account (ideally a live account!) with a good brokerage.

There are essentially two types of broker:

Dealing desk / Market maker

Non-dealing desk / ECN / STP

During our careers as traders and analysts, we have found that the best kind of brokerage is a "non-dealing desk" brokerage as they do not trade against you and are, therefore, more interested in your success.

Dealing desk brokers, by contrast, are more interested in your failure as every dollar you lose is a dollar they win.

Of course, even within the realms of non-dealing desk brokerages, the quality can vary tremendously and, for that reason, within the member area of our website is a list of brokers that we use and recommend based on their excellent service, fast trade execution, narrow spreads, etc.

All of our recommended brokers offer you the option of opening a live account **and** a demo account, so that you can gain experience with MetaTrader and the strategies you will learn later in this book before risking your own money.

We always suggest that you open both types of account with whichever of our recommended brokerages appeals to you, especially if you are just beginning with FOREX but, if you are more experienced, then you may simply wish to open a live account. Regardless of your situation, you will find that trading with a quality brokerage will make your overall experience that much better.

No matter which brokerage you ultimately select, you will be able to download MetaTrader 4 - this *free* application combines your charting program and your trading platform in one easy-to-use system.

MetaTrader 4 is very intuitive to use, allows trades to be placed directly from the charts, supports many languages, has a comprehensive in-built help system plus many more features than we could possibly have time to describe in this book.

CHAPTER 9
ABOUT METATRADER 4

MetaTrader 4 (MT4) is an on-line trading system designed to provide broker services to customers for FOREX, Futures and CFD markets. This is a "whole-cycle" complex, which means that you will not need any other software to organize your broker services if using MetaTrader 4.

More about MT 4 can be found here: http://www.metaquotes.net/metatrader

There are several types of MT 4 software but the main variants are:

MetaTrader 4 Terminal. You will learn about this version of MetaTrader 4 in this book

MetaTrader 4 Mobile. Maintains technical analysis, charting, news and offers live trading via PDAs, SmartPhones, etc. from almost anywhere in the world.

Mobile trading (m-trading) — controlling a trading account via mobile devices such as cellular phones or PDAs (Personal Digital Assistants). Wireless Access Technologies WAP (http://www.metaquotes.net/wap) and GPRS provide access to the Internet.

Unfortunately, MetaTrader4 Mobile is generally something you need to pay for but some brokerages now offer it free like the main terminal application. You can read about it here if you feel it may be useful for you: http://www.metaquotes.net/mobile_terminals

Downloading and Installing MetaTrader 4

Downloading MetaTrader 4

Depending on your chosen brokerage, download and installation instructions for MetaTrader 4 will either be sent to you by e-mail or presented on a download page after registering – this is a free, no obligation process so do not worry about it.

> *Note: MetaTrader 4 is compatible with Microsoft Windows 98/ME/2000/XP/2003/Vista & Windows 7, **not Windows 95**. It can run on a Mac if Windows emulation software in installed.*

Installing MetaTrader 4

After downloading the setup program (usually named something like "mt4setup.exe") to your PC, run it and follow the on-screen instructions to complete the installation process. **Write down the installation folder location as you will need that later**.

When launching the program for the first time, you will see a window containing a registration form. After you have completed that, you will automatically be issued with a demo account.

Configuring MetaTrader 4

The trading system we use has been created with MetaTrader 4. Keep in mind that the same technical indicators and settings may give different results on different trade terminals and/or with different technical analysis software.

If you particularly want (or need) to trade with a different platform (or your current brokerage does not support MetaTrader 4) then you can open a demo account with one of our recommended brokerages and run both systems in parallel while you identify any variations between the two systems.

Now we will move on to configuring MetaTrader 4 to look as it appears in the following screenshots.

Starting MetaTrader 4 for the first time

After first starting MT4, you will see a screen similar to the image below:

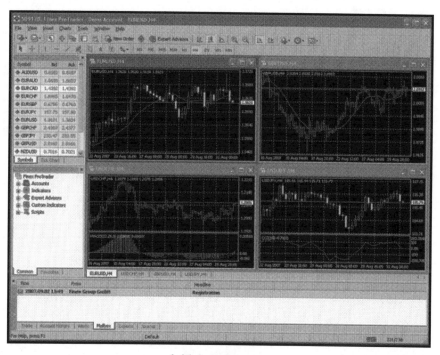

Initial workspace

Then, the registration window (as shown on the next page) will appear in the middle of that workspace.

Opening a demo account

The "**Open an Account**" dialog enables you to open a demo account.

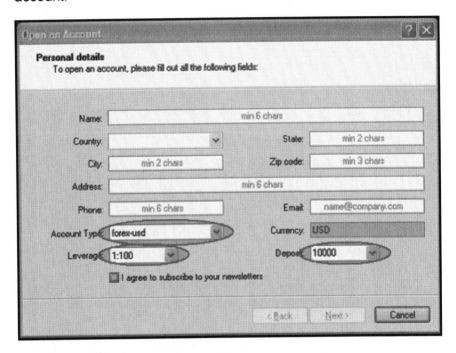

Note: Some versions of MetaTrader have a different "Account Type" description, as shown below, but all work in the same basic way – the default is usually a dollar-designated account.

You may wish to adjust the Leverage and Deposit amounts but "1:100" and "$10,000" will be perfectly adequate for our purposes, especially if you are just learning about FOREX, as it will enable you to follow the examples in this course more easily.

Once you have entered your details, click the "**Next**" button to move on to the Trading Servers dialog:

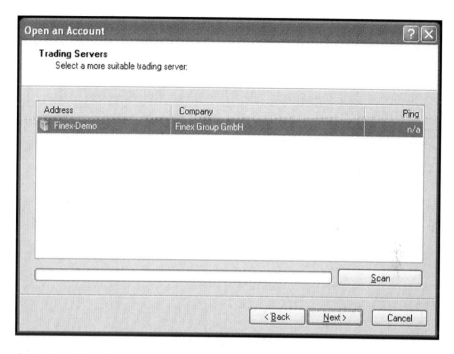

Click the "**Next**" button to select the default server:

And finally, click the "**Finish**" button.

All done! You have created your first demo account.

The next thing to do is configure the layout of **MetaTrader 4**.

The following pages will show you how to do this and also how to apply and use the indicators that we need to trade the system.

An auto-installer application is available from the member area of the www.EvolvedForexTrading.com website and will install all of the relevant files quickly and easily.

Adjusting the workspace of MetaTrader 4

By now, you should see the workspace of MT4 looking something like this:

As you can see in the left hand "**Navigator**" panel, the account details have appeared.

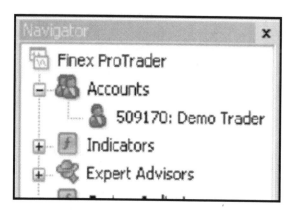

At the same time, below the workspace in the "**Mailbox**" page, you can see the message from the brokerage. It will contain details of your demo account registration:

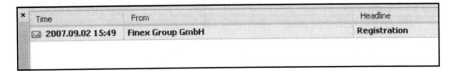

If you double-click (with your left mouse button) on the title of the message then it will open and you will be able to read it:

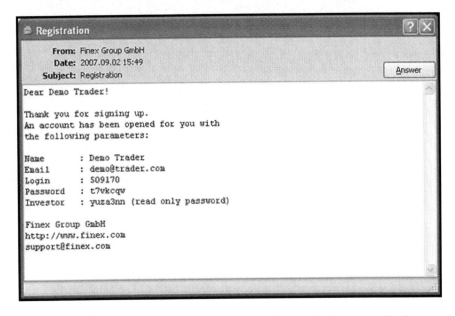

In future, you can refer to this message to remind yourself of your account details.

Setting up Chart Windows and Indicators

You are looking at the default appearance of the chart windows.

We do not want to use the default profile so we need to create our own, personal one.

To begin with, we need to create "**Templates**" and, after that, by specifying these "**Templates**", create our own "**Profile**".

To save some time, and avoid cluttering this book with the full process, we will use the existing templates that we have provided:

- one for a 15-minute chart, and

- one for a 60-minute chart.

These "**Templates**" will help us to create our "**5emas**" profile.

For more information on creating **"Templates"** and **"Profiles"**, review the **"Help System"** within MT4, as shown.

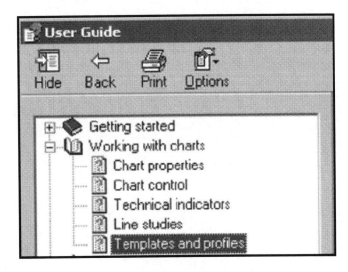

Part of what we will be doing before creating a profile is adjusting the size and position of the chart windows. After that, all of our new settings will be saved automatically each time we modify the profile.

Ok! Time to get started!

The first thing to consider is the size and resolution of your computer screen.

If your screen is quite small or has a low resolution (anything less than 1024x768 is impractical for trading) then we will need to "create" some space by deleting the "GBPUSD" chart window. That chart is not really required as we will be concentrating on the other three displayed currency pairs ("USDJPY", "EURUSD" and "USDCHF").

Once you have decided how many of the initial 4 charts you wish to retain, we need to create secondary copies of each. This is because we will be working with both 60-minute and 15-minute charts for each currency pair traded.

You should now have 3 or 4 chart windows: "USDJPY", "EURUSD", "USDCHF" and possibly "GBPUSD".

Next, open a secondary chart for each of the current charts by first clicking the "New Chart" button (shown below), then selecting the required currency pair.

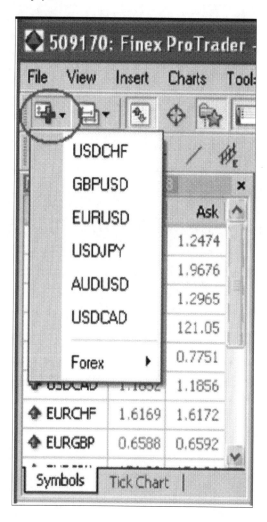

When you have finished, your screen will probably be a mess of charts.

Not to worry – just click the "Window" menu and select "Tile Vertically".

You will then have a chart area looking something like this:

As we stated before, if you have a small or low resolution screen then you may well find the chart display to be cramped and/or difficult to read. If so, delete the "GBPUSD" charts and re-tile the window.

The other thing you will have noticed is that the charts are in no particular order but, that too, is easily remedied. The chart windows behave just like regular MS-Windows windows so you can simply drag them into the correct positions.

An alternative approach (since the chart windows will be nicely positioned already) is to click and drag the required currency pair from the "Market Watch" list on the left and drop it onto an existing chart. This will change the currency pair of that chart to whatever currency pair you dragged from the Market Watch window.

Depending on the number of charts you have displayed (and your personal preference), you may find it better to arrange your charts either side-by-side or one-above-the-other.

Your final arrangement should look something like this:

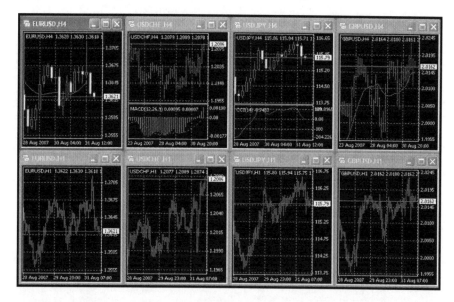

Ok! Our chart positioning is done – the next step is to set the timeframes.

If you arranged your charts side-by-side then we suggest you make the left-hand chart of each pair your 60-minute chart. If they are one-above-the-other then make the top row your 60-minute charts.

Select each chart in turn and then click either the "H1" or "M15" button in the toolbar (you may also wish to zoom in or out for a better view).

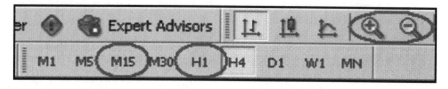

If you have not done so already, please download and install the 5 EMAs templates.

There are two pre-prepared "**MT4 Templates**":

"5emas_15" - the template for 15-minute charts
"5emas_60" - the template for 60-minute charts

Copy both files to the "templates" folder of your MT4 installation – hopefully you remembered to write down the location when you installed MT4. If not, simply hover your mouse over the MT4 icon on your Windows Desktop and the location will be displayed in a small "hint" panel.

For each chart in turn, right-click your mouse within the chart window and select **Template** from the context menu.

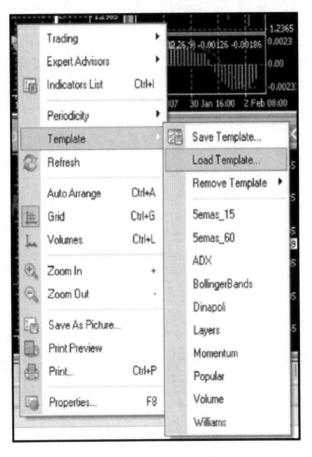

If the "5emas" templates appear in the list then simply select the correct one. If not, select **Load Template**, in which case, a standard Windows "Open" dialog will appear:

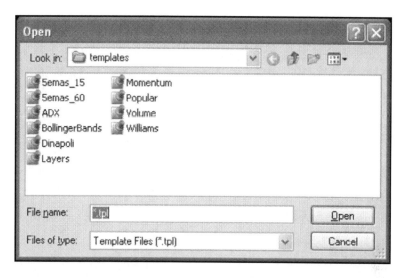

Depending upon the chart you have selected, you will need to choose the "**5emas_15.tpl**" or "**5emas_60.tpl**" template then click the "**Open**" button.

This will change the way each chart appears and will also apply the correct technical indicators for you, as you can see:

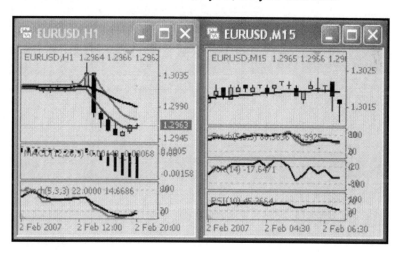

The final step is simply to save the new layout as a profile.

Click **File->Profiles->Save As...** and the following dialog will appear:

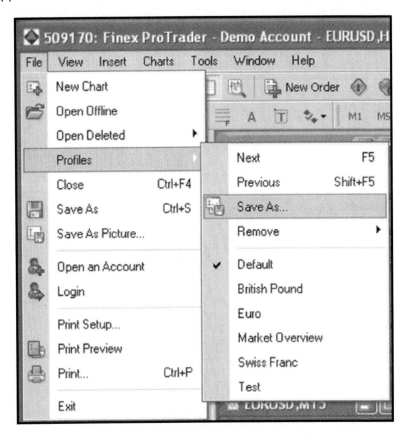

Enter the name of the profile, for example "**Evolved - 5EMAs**"and click "**Ok**".

Your profile is now stored and will be loaded by default each time you open MetaTrader 4.

As you become more experienced, you will probably wish to create additional profiles. Saved profiles can be recalled at any time so this makes it very quick and convenient to switch between different chart views.

MetaTrader 4 configuration is now complete and we are ready to move on to the **Main FOREX System** itself.

CHAPTER 10
TRADING RULES FOR THE MAIN
FOREX SYSTEM-"Day-Trading"

The Main Set of Rules (fundamental)

Do not trade before important fundamental news!

Please refer to the section on **"Fundamental Analysis"** for clarification.

You should be patient and wait for a market set-up that occurs **after** news has been released.

It is fair to assume that a news release could pull the market up or down and so you should wait for the market to pullback before looking for trade alerts to occur.

If you already have an open position that is in profit, we strongly suggest that you close it prior to any important fundamental news release.

We also suggest that you trade very carefully on Fridays and the days running up to the end of a month, quarter or year.

A little more sage advice if you are new to the FOREX markets...

Before starting to trade the **"MAIN FOREX SYSTEM"** with real money, we strongly recommend that you practice with a demo account until you can reliably identify winning setups. Our usual suggestion is that you switch to trading a live account **after** you have traded a demo account profitably for a whole month.

Finally, we also recommend you study our other trading course – **Essential Fibonacci and Divergence Strategies** (available soon) which enhances and compliments the MAIN FOREX SYSTEM strategy.

We believe the **Essential Fibonacci and Divergence Strategies** is a "Must Read" for traders of all levels as the methods both for adapting the Main strategy and for trading divergences that are described in that course apply very much to the standard **"MAIN FOREX SYSTEM"** you are about to learn.

IMPORTANT!

Before we proceed, allow us to apologize in advance for what might appear to be constant repetition.

The reason for this is that the strategy rules for long and short entries/exits are simply the reverse of each other and we wanted to provide a suitable quantity of examples.

NOTE:

As we mentioned previously, this trading system is flexible so it could equally qualify as a day-trading, short-term or even scalping system. How you implement it is your choice.

Similarly, if you are a conservative trader and only use the system with Exit Strategy 1 then you will close half each position at 25 pips profit and let the other half run until it hopefully reaches 50 pips within 24 hours, therefore counting yourself a day-trader and adopting the system as day-trading system.

If, on the other hand, you see reason to keep positions open for perhaps as long as 3 days by using Exit Strategies 2 and 3 then you automatically turn the system into short-term system.

In an attempt to avoid confusion, we have prepared trading plans for different types of traders - please refer to the Appendix at the end of this book for more details.

The Main Rules (technical)

Entry Rules for Short Positions:

- The MACD (1-Hr chart) must have been below the zero line for at least 3 bars.

  The earliest entry point is the 4th consecutive bar below the zero line.

- Wait for price to touch the 5 period EMA of the Highs (turquoise line).

  As we can see in the following illustration, price did not touch the turquoise line until the 5th MACD bar.

- Ideally, wait for the Stochastic on the 1-hour chart to indicate an overbought situation (value ≥ 80).

- Ideally, wait for the Stochastic on the 15-minute chart to indicate an overbought situation (value ≥ 80).

- Ideally, wait for the Williams' %R on the 15-minute chart to indicate an overbought situation (value ≥ -20).

- Ideally, wait for the RSI on the 15-minute chart to indicate an overbought situation (value ≥ 70).

Additional information:

If the entry signal occurs at a time when price is below the 20 period EMA of the Closes (black line on the 1-Hr chart), as in the illustration below, this indicates a much stronger trade alert.

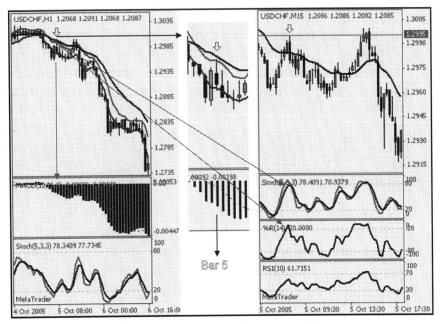

20 period EMA of the Closes as a filter

Entry Rules for Long Positions:

- The MACD (1-Hr chart) must have been above the zero line for at least 3 bars.

  The earllest entry point is the 4th consecutive bar above the zero line.

- Wait for price to touch the 5 period EMA of the Lows (maroon line).

  As we can see in the following illustration, price did not touch the maroon line until the 4th MACD bar.

- Ideally, wait for the Stochastic on the 1-hour chart to indicate an oversold situation (value ≤ 20).

- Ideally, wait for the Stochastic on the 15-minute chart to indicate an oversold situation (value ≤ 20).

- Ideally, wait for the Williams' %R on the 15-minute chart to indicate an oversold situation (value ≤ -80).

- Ideally, wait for the RSI on the 15-minute chart to indicate an oversold situation (value ≤ 30).

Additional information:

If the entry signal occurs at a time when price is above the 20 period EMA of the Closes (black line on the 1-Hr chart), as in the illustration below, this indicates a much stronger trade alert.

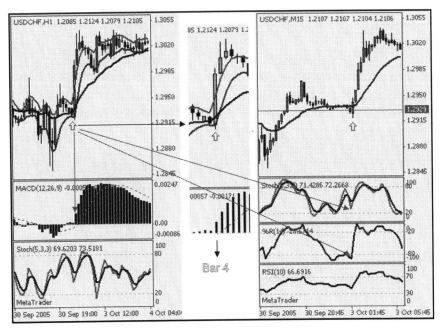

A much stronger trade alert

As you can hopefully see, understanding the rules for buy and sell alerts is very easy.

Now let us consider the rules for exiting trade positions.

There are three exit strategies for this system.

100

All 3 Exit Strategies

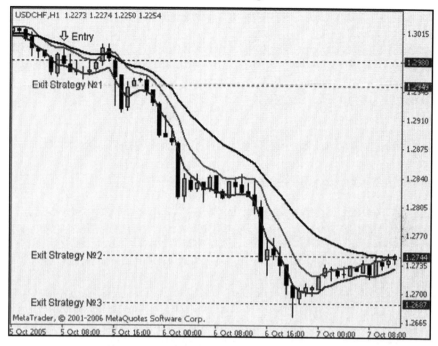

Exit Strategies

In the following examples, we will be opening positions consisting of two 0.1 lot orders.

So, time to push on and consider the exit strategies in detail:

Exit Rules for Short Positions

We have already briefly covered Exit Strategy №1 in the "**General Money Management Rules for the Main FOREX System**" section of this book but now it is time to examine it (and the two alternatives) more closely.

> *Note: On the next page, we will split the image above into three parts, so that everything will be easier to understand.*

First, however, we need to open our positions:

Open two 0.1 lot short positions from **1.2980**, **Stop Losses** @ 45 pips = **1.3025**

Take Profit for one position @ 31 pips = **1.2949**

The next few pages will go through some detailed examples of the exit strategies used in this trading system so that you can follow the mechanics clearly:

Exit Strategy №1 (Trailing Stop method 1)

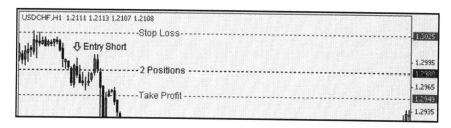

Rules

When price reaches **1.2949**, the **Take Profit** closes the first position automatically but the second position remains open.

At this point, we need to move the **Stop Loss** for the second position to the entry (break-even) level, i.e. **1.2980**.

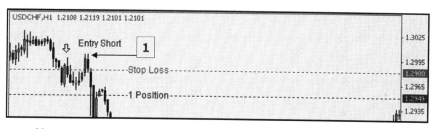

Note:
Although we have a higher high/low [marker 1] after entering the trade, this did not trigger the Stop Loss because it was still at 1.3025 - we only moved the Stop Loss after price fell to 1.2949 (green line).

Now, if the remaining position gains another 30-35 pips (down to **1.2919-1.2914** in our case) then simply move the **Stop Loss** the same distance.

Repeat this step each time the remaining position gains an additional 30-35 pips profit until, eventually, the position will be closed by the **Stop Loss**.

Exit Strategy №1 (Trailing Stop method 2)

Rules

When price reaches **1.2949**, the **Take Profit** closes the first position automatically but the second position remains open.

Once the first position has been automatically closed, wait until price forms a second high.

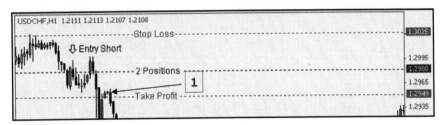

When that occurs, move the **Stop Loss** for the second position to 5 pips above the high of that price bar i.e. to **1.2964** as the high of that price bar is 1.2959.

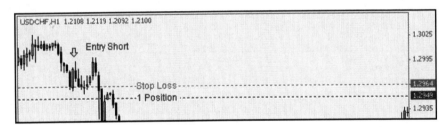

Now, if the remaining position gains another 30-35 pips (down to **1.2934-1.2929** in our case) then simply move the **Stop Loss** the same distance.

Repeat this step each time the remaining position gains an additional 30-35 pips profit until, eventually, the position will be closed by the **Stop Loss**.

As you can see, there is nothing difficult with either version of Exit Strategy №1 and you will be pleased to know that Exit Strategy №2 is even easier!

Exit Strategy №2 (Moving Averages)

This really is very easy. You simply follow the 20 period EMA of the Closes.

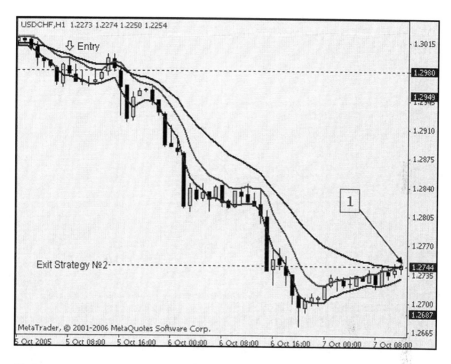

Rules

Keep the remaining position open until a price bar closes above all three moving averages **[marker 1]** as detailed in the magnified sections of chart below showing the exit price bar closing above the moving averages and what happened next:

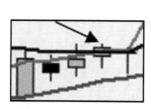

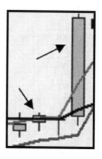

If desired, you can back-up this exit strategy using the standard **Trailing Stop** feature built into **Meta Trader 4**.

Exit Strategy №3 (Using Divergences)

Here we will take a bullish divergence as our cue to exit the remaining position.

Please look at the following illustration:

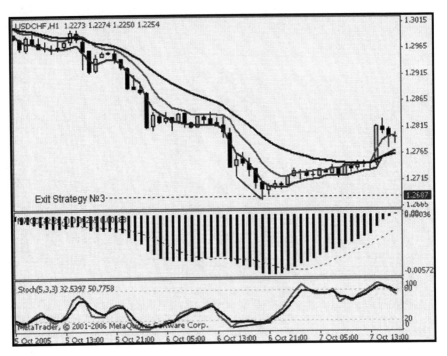

Rules

We need to watch out for divergences between the price levels and the indicators (MACD and Stochastic). In this instance, we cannot see anything on the MACD, but a bullish divergence is clearly visible on the Stochastic.

Since we have a clear indication of an oversold condition, we can exit safely on this divergence.

Exit Rules for Long Positions

As you should expect, they follow the same rules as for short positions, just in reverse.

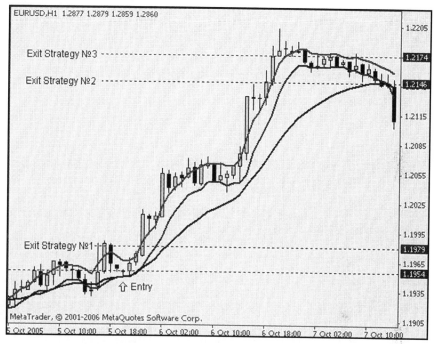

> **Note**: On the next page, we will split the above image into three parts so that everything will be easier to understand.

Before starting, we need to open our positions

Open two 0.1 lot positions from **1.1954**, **Stop Losses** @ 45 pips = **1.1909**

Take Profit for one position @ 25 pips = **1.1979**

> **Note:** The Take Profit distance shown above is different to the Short Position examples earlier but can you think why that is? Simply because this is a GBPUSD example and the $/pip value is different!

> **Remember:** The objective with our first position is to hit our daily profit target and use the second position for bonus profits.

Exit Strategy №1 (Trailing Stop method 1)

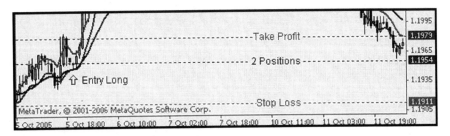

Rules

When price reaches **1.1979**, the **Take Profit** closes the first position automatically but the second position remains open.

At this point, we need to move the **Stop Loss** for the second position to the entry (break-even) level, i.e. **1.1954**.

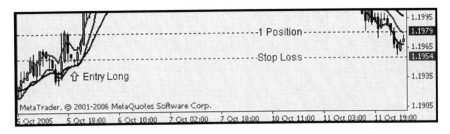

Now, if the remaining position gains another 30-35 pips (up to **1.2009-1.2014** in our case) then simply move the **Stop Loss** the same distance.

Repeat this step each time the remaining position gains an additional 30-35 pips profit until, eventually, the position will be closed by the **Stop Loss**.

Exit Strategy №1 (Trailing Stop method 2)

Rules

When price reaches **1.1979**, the **Take Profit** closes the first position automatically but the second position remains open

Once the first position has been automatically closed, wait until price forms a second low **[marker 1]**.

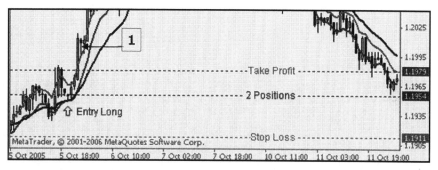

Figure:

Now move the **Stop Loss** for the second position to 5 pips below the low of that price bar i.e. to **1.1986** as the low of that price bar is 1.1991.

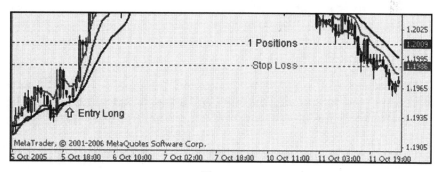

Figure:

As the remaining position gains the next 30-35 pips (up to **1.2009-1.2014** in our case), simply move the **Stop Loss** the same distance and repeat for each 30-35 pips gained until, eventually, the position will be closed by the **Stop Loss**.

There is nothing difficult about the Exit Strategy №1 approaches but Exit Strategy №2 is less involved, i.e. it is more mechanical.

Exit Strategy №2 (Moving Averages)

As before, simply follow the 20 period EMA of the Closes.

Rules

Keep the remaining position open until a price bar closes below all three moving averages **[marker 1]**. Below is the magnified chart segment showing the close signal and what happened next:

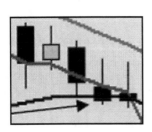

As mentioned previously, you are free to implement a **Trailing Stop** as an additional way to protect/maximize profits and that a standard **Trailing Stop** feature is built into **MetaTrader 4**.

Exit Strategy №3 (Using of Divergences)

In this example, we will be using a bearish divergence to signal our exit of the remaining position.

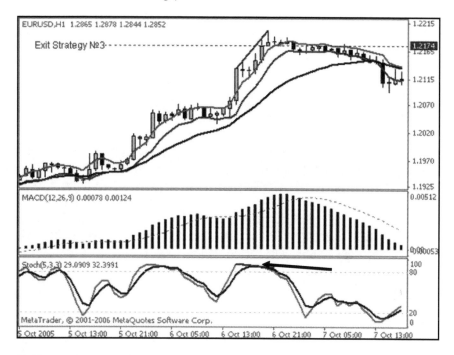

Rules

We need to watch out for divergences between the price levels and the indicators (MACD and Stochastic). As before, we cannot see anything on the MACD but a bearish divergence is clearly visible on the Stochastic (Marked by arrow).

As we have clear indication of an overbought condition, we can exit safely on this divergence.

It is now down to you to decide which exit strategies you wish to use. All three are relatively simple but you will need to practice

Strategy №3 until you become proficient at identifying the divergence points.

Ideal Technical Conditions for Opening Positions

There are many, many opportunities to trade with this system but, as you should suspect, some opportunities will be better than others and some will be almost perfect.

The biggest issue for many traders (not just of this system) is learning what to look for and developing an ability to filter out those poorer entries.

Some strategies are almost unbelievably complex which makes it extremely difficult for new users to even understand the rudiments of the system, let alone develop an eye for good potential entries.

Fortunately, the rules for our strategy are very straightforward, allowing new traders to quickly understand the system. This lets them spend less time with the strategy mechanics and more time gaining the skill to identify the best entries, thereby increasing their win rate.

With the above in mind, we will consider the **ideal** technical conditions for opening both long and short positions with a high probability of successful trades. Of course, the very best way to achieve this is with some illustrations and explanations.

Ideal conditions for SHORT positions

USD/CHF

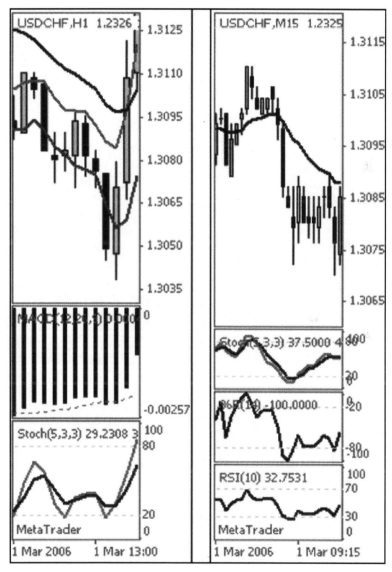

Trade 1

Trade 1 (Hypothetical profit is 61 pips in 8 hours)

USD/CHF

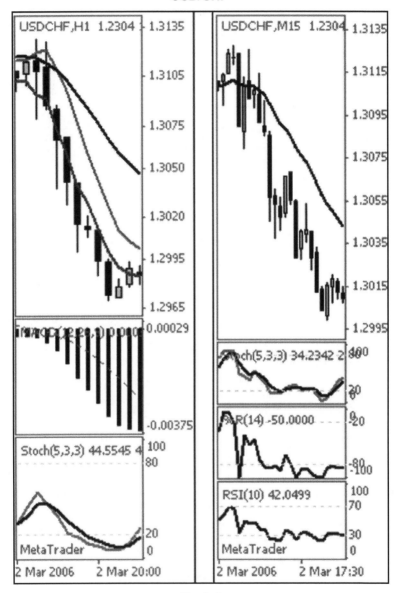

Trade 2

Trade 2 (Hypothetical profit is 131 pips in 9 hours)

Trade 1 (USD/CHF)

1)   The 5 period EMA of the Highs is below the 20 period EMA of the Closes – the best circumstances for us!

2)   Price makes a small break-through of the 5 period EMA of the Highs **and** the 20 period EMA on the Closes.

3)   The MACD has been below the zero line for some time and the Stochastic is above the 50% level indicating a move toward an overbought condition.

4)   On the 15-minute chart, Stochastic, Williams' %R and RSI are all indicating an overbought condition.

Trade 2 (USD/CHF)

1)   The 5 period EMA of the Highs is below the 20 period EMA of the Closes – the best circumstances for us!

2)   Price makes a small break-through of the 5 period EMA of the Highs **and** the 20 period EMA on the Closes.

3)   The MACD has been below the zero line for some time but stronger downward movement is beginning to develop and the Stochastic is in middle-ground.

4)   On the 15-minute chart, Stochastic, Williams' %R and RSI are all indicating an overbought condition.

USD/JPY

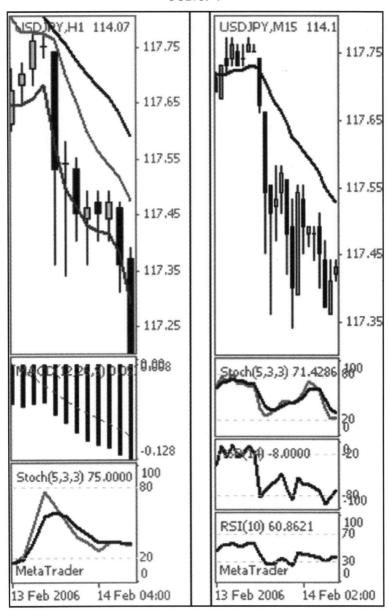

Trade 3

Trade 3 (Hypothetical profit is 47 pips in 7 hours)

USD/JPY

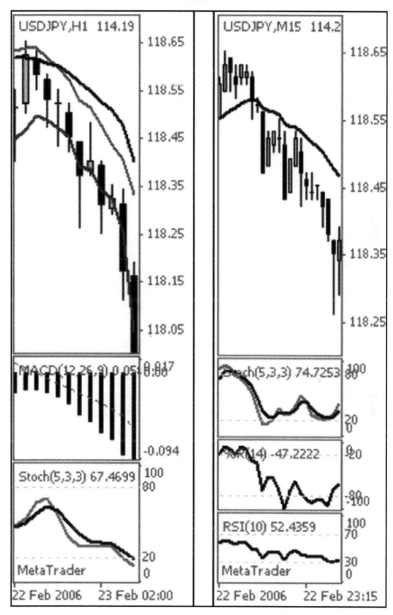

Trade 4

Trade 4 (Hypothetical profit is 155 pips in 18 hours)

Trade 3 (USD/JPY)

1)   The 5 period EMA of the Highs is below the 20 period EMA of the Closes – a strong confirmation!

2)   There is a clear pull-back of price to the 5 period EMA of the Highs.

3)   The MACD is below the zero line and the Stochastic almost indicating an overbought condition.

4)   On the 15-minute chart, Stochastic, Williams' %R and RSI are all indicating an overbought condition.

Trade 4 (USD/JPY)

1)   The 5 period EMA of the Highs is below the 20 period EMA of the Closes – a strong confirmation!

2)   Price makes a small break-through of the 5 period EMA of the Highs.

3)   The MACD is below the zero line and stronger downward movement is beginning to develop while the Stochastic is in the middle-upper region.

4)   On the 15-minute chart, Stochastic, Williams' %R and RSI are all indicating an overbought condition.

EUR/USD

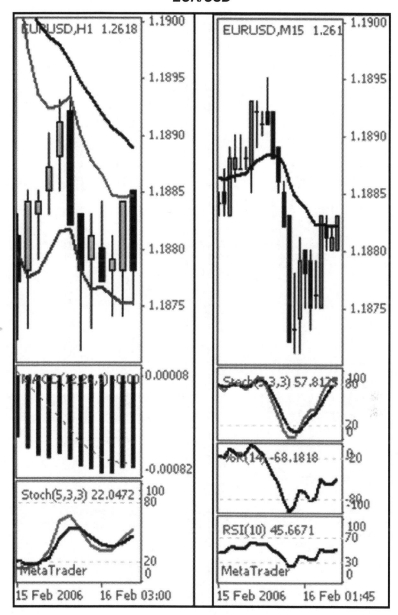

Trade 5

Trade 5 (Hypothetical profit is 40 pips in 12 hours)

EUR/USD

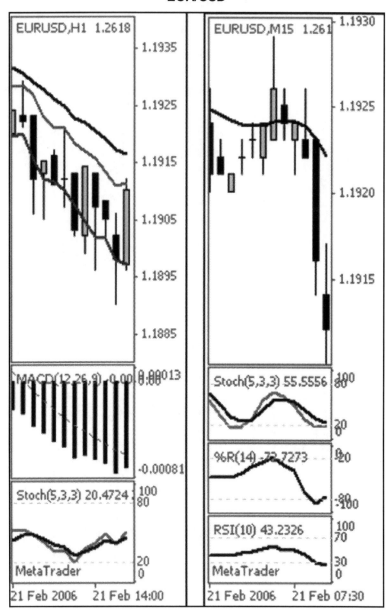

Trade 6

Trade 6 (Hypothetical profit is 56 pips in 28 hours)

Trade 5 (EUR/USD)

1) The 5 period EMA of the Highs is below the 20 period EMA of the Closes – a strong confirmation!

2) Price makes a small break-through of the 5 period EMA of the Highs.

3) The MACD is below the zero line and the Stochastic almost indicating an overbought condition.

4) On the 15-minute chart, Stochastic, Williams' %R and RSI are all indicating an overbought condition.

Trade 6 (EUR/USD)

1) The 5 period EMA of the Highs is below the 20 period EMA of the Closes – a strong confirmation!

2) Price makes a small break-through of the 5 period EMA of the Highs.

3) The MACD is below the zero line with downward movement beginning to develop and the Stochastic in middle-ground.

4) On the 15-minute chart, Stochastic and Williams' %R (though not RSI) are indicating an overbought condition.

This section has concentrated on ideal conditions for short positions so now we will move on to long positions.

Ideal conditions for LONG positions

USD/CHF

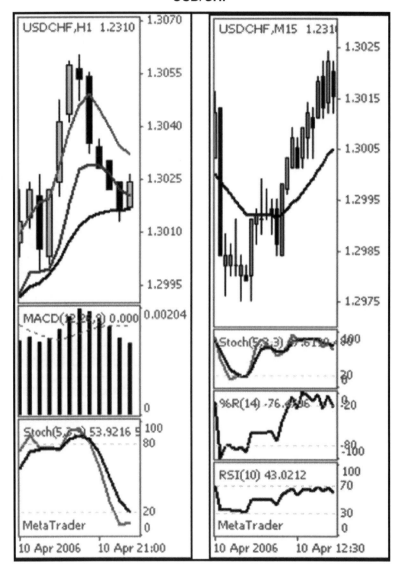

Trade 1

Trade 1 (Hypothetical profit is 60 pips in 3 hours)

USD/CHF

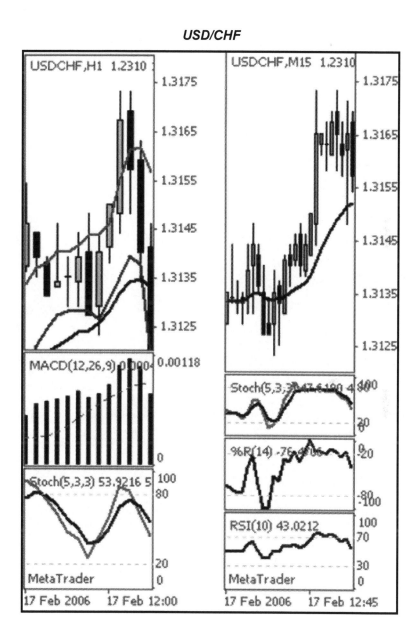

Trade 2

Trade 2 (Hypothetical profit is 44 pips in 3 hours)

Trade 1 (USD/CHF)

1)   The 5 period EMA of the Lows is above the 20 period EMA of the Closes – a strong confirmation!

2)   There is a clear pull-back of price to the 5 period EMA of the Lows.

3)   The MACD is above the zero line and, although the Stochastic is indicating an overbought condition, prior to entering the trade it had fallen to below 80.

4)   On the 15-minute chart, Stochastic and Williams' %R (though not RSI) are indicating an oversold condition.

Trade 2 (USD/CHF)

1)   The 5 period EMA of the Lows is above the 20 period EMA of the Closes – a strong confirmation!

2)   There is a clear pull-back of price to the 5 period EMA of the Lows.

3)   The MACD is above the zero line and the Stochastic is almost in the oversold region (value is about 20).

4)   On the 15-minute chart, Stochastic and Williams' %R (though not RSI) are indicating an oversold condition.

USD/JPY

Trade 3

Trade 3 (Hypothetical profit is 35 pips in 8 hours)

USD/JPY

Trade 4

Trade 4 (Hypothetical profit is 80 pips in 6 hours)

Trade 3 (USD/JPY)

1)   The 5 period EMA of the Lows is above the 20 period EMA of the Closes – a strong confirmation!

2)   Price makes a small break-through of the 5 period EMA of the Lows.

3)   The MACD is above the zero line and the Stochastic is in middle-ground.

4)   On the 15-minute chart, Williams' %R is indicating an oversold condition, RSI is in middle-ground and Stochastic is showing a bullish divergence.

Trade 4 (USD/JPY)

1)   The 5 period EMA of the Lows is above the 20 period EMA of the Closes – a strong confirmation!

2)   Price makes a small break-through of the 5 period EMA of the Lows.

3)   The MACD is above the zero line and the Stochastic is in middle-ground (but quite close to oversold territory).

4)   On the 15-minute chart, only the Williams' %R is indicating an oversold condition but we have the Stochastic from the 1-Hr chart to back it up, which is actually a better confirmation for us.

EUR/USD

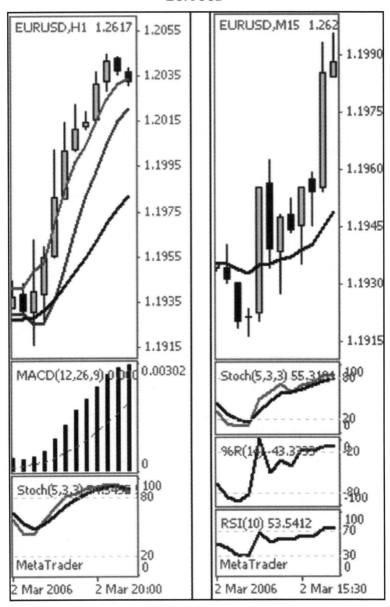

Trade 5

Trade 5 (Hypothetical profit is 100 pips in 8 hours)

EUR/USD

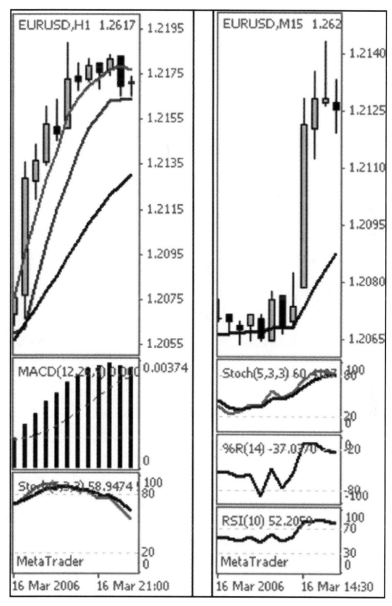

Trade 6

Trade 6 (Hypothetical profit is 100 pips in 5 hours)

Trade 5 (EUR/USD)

1) The 5 period EMA of the Lows is above the 20 period EMA of the Closes – a strong confirmation!

2) There is a clear pull-back of price to the 5 period EMA of the Lows.

3) The MACD is above the zero line and looks to be moving further upward and the Stochastic is in middle-ground.

4) On the 15-minute chart, Stochastic, Williams' %R and RSI are all indicating an oversold condition.

Trade 6 (EUR/USD)

1) The 5 period EMA of the Lows is above the 20 period EMA of the Closes – a strong confirmation!

2) There is a clear pull-back of price to the 5 period EMA of the Lows.

3) The MACD is above the zero line and the Stochastic is in upper-ground.

4) On the 15-minute chart, Stochastic, Williams' %R and RSI are all indicating an oversold condition.

To conclude this section, we have three more charts. Two (USD/CHF and EUR/USD) showing ideal trade set-ups with trade opportunities lasting for several consecutive price bars and, to show how simple this strategy can be, these entry examples completely ignore the 15-minute chart.

Finally, we show a series of possible trade entries for **USD/JPY:**

Two ideal trade setups

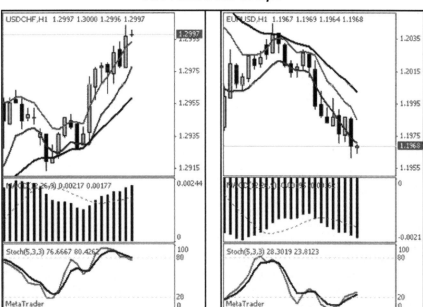

Ideal long and short trade setups

USD/CHF

1)   The 5 period EMA of the Lows is above the 20 period EMA of the Closes – a strong confirmation!

2)   There are several clear pull-backs of price through the 5 period EMA of the Lows.

3)   The MACD is above the zero line and the Stochastic is in lower-ground.

EUR/USD

1)   The 5 period EMA of the Highs is below the 20 period EMA of the Closes – a strong confirmation!

2)   There are several clear pull-backs of price through the 5 period EMA of the Highs.

3)   The MACD is below the zero line and the Stochastic is in upper-ground.

A series of possible trade entries

USDJPY,H1 113.73 113.97 113.71 113.86

MACD(12,26,9) 0.160 0.147

Stoch(5,3,3) 47.8887 56.5575

UniTrade

7 Jun 2006   7 Jun 13:00   7 Jun 21:00   8 Jun 05:00

5 serial trades

If you missed the initial entry point **[marker 1]** then you could try again **[marker 2]**, and again **[marker 3]**, and again **[marker 4]** and again **[marker 5]** (in fact, marker 5 represents an area with **three** additional opportunities to enter!). Once you begin trading this strategy, you will see the **USD/JPY** currency pair do this quite frequently. ☺

In this last section we have looked at ideal trade opportunities for both long and short positions, but that is only half of the story.

It is now time to consider what most courses <u>fail to explain</u>... the market conditions when it is better to stand aside and preserve your capital.

When Not To Enter the Market ("No Trade" Rules)

For every trading system there will (or should) be exceptions to the rules.

Even though the system you are trading may be giving you trade entry signals, there are some fundamental and technical market conditions that should ring very loud alarm bells and prompt you **not to trade**.

Let us look at some examples:

Exceptions based on fundamental events (news)

As we have already explained, you should not open positions before important fundamental news, even though a system may be giving you a trade signal.

If you already have positions open then you are normally best to close them if possible (especially if they are in profit) – at the very least you should move your Stop Loss to a more appropriate level.

Look at these two examples of what a news report can do and how you can be adversely affected if you have open trades when certain news is released.

These two examples will definitely be enough to get our point across.

EUR/USD

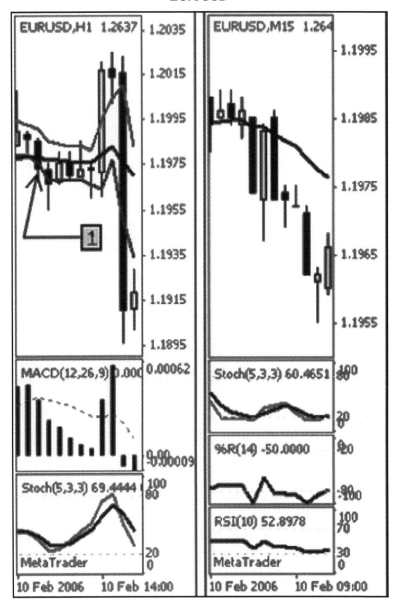

Trade1

Trade 1 (EUR/USD long)

USD/CHF

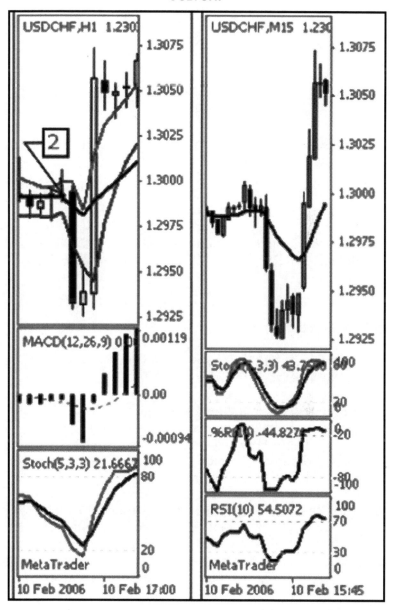

Trade 2 Short

Trade 1 (EUR/USD long)

Here we have a good opportunity to open a long position. Look at the price bar of the entry point **[marker 1]**.

1)   The 5 period EMA of the Lows is a little lower than the 20 period EMA of the Closes but we have other good signals (see points 2, 3 & 4 below).

2)   There is a pull-back of price to the 5 period EMA of the Lows and also a small break-through.

3)   The MACD is above the zero line and the Stochastic on the 60-minute chart is indicating oversold.

4)   On the 15-minute chart, Stochastic and Williams' %R (though not RSI) are indicating an oversold condition.

Trade 1 (description)

Our entry point is 1.1975 for 2 x 1.0 lot orders. Stop Losses @ 1.1935. Take Profit for one order @ 1.2000.

According to our trading rules, when price rose to 1.2000, the Take Profit would have automatically closed our first order and banked us 25 pips. We would then have moved the Stop Loss for the remaining order to the entry point (1.1975) and waited for an exit signal. That is all very good in theory...

...but, after the news is released, the market plummets and, although the Stop Loss would trigger an exit to take us out of the market, it is highly unlikely that we would exit at our requested price level. In such a fast-moving market, the price we actually exited at could be anywhere between the price we wanted (1.1975) and the low of that price bar (about 1.1895). In monetary terms, that means a real cash loss on the remaining position of **up to $800!** Even offsetting the profit from the first order, we would still be out of pocket by as much as $550 which effectively puts us three days behind in our 12-month plan.

Trade 2 (USD/CHF short)

Here we have good opportunity to open a short position. See the price bar of the entry point [marker 2].

1)   The 5 period EMA of the Highs is a little higher than the 20 period EMA of the Closes [marker 2] but we have other good signals (see points 2, 3 & 4 below).

2)   There is a pull-back of price to the 5 period EMA of the Highs and also a small break-through.

3)   The MACD is below the zero line and the Stochastic on the 60-minute chart is in middle-ground.

4)   On the 15-minute chart, Stochastic, Williams' %R and RSI are indicating an overbought condition.

Trade 2 (description)

Our entry point is 1.3000 for 2 x 1.0 lot orders. Stop Losses @ 1.3045. Take Profit for one order @ 1.2975.

Following our trading rules, when price fell to 1.2975 the Take Profit would have automatically closed our first position and banked us 25 pips. We would then have moved the Stop Loss for the remaining position to the entry point (1.3000). Once again, all looked great in theory!

After the news is announced, the market surges upward and our second position is closed by the Stop Loss. As in the previous example, the potential loss for that remaining position is anywhere between $0 and $750.

We hope you now understand why it is better not to trade before a fundamental news release.

Now we can look at some examples of unwanted technical conditions.

Exceptions based on technical conditions

As before, just two examples should help you to understand.

USD/JPY

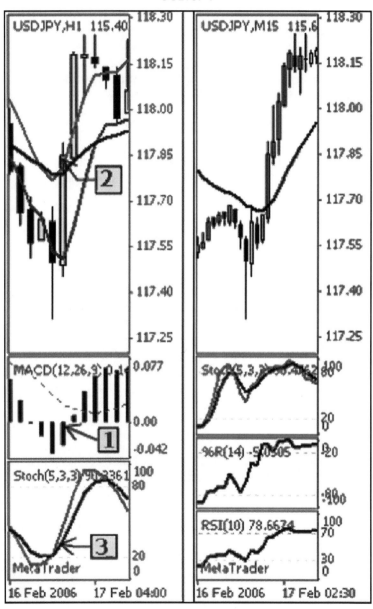

Trade 1

USD/CHF

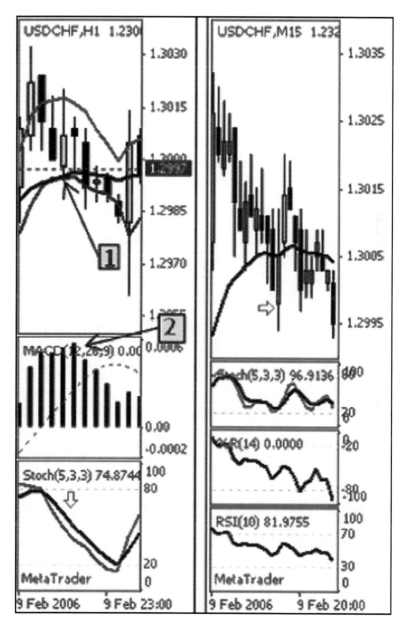

Trade 2

Trade 1 (USD/JPY short)

In this instance, we would not open any positions at all. The third bar of the MACD has closed below the zero line [marker 1] but price has closed higher than all three EMAs [marker 2]. In addition, the Stochastic has begun moving out of the oversold zone [marker 3].

This example should need no further commentary!

Trade 2 (USD/CHF long)

Here we have a good opportunity to open a long position at the 1.2997 level - see the price bar of the entry point [marker 1].

1) The 5 period EMA of the Lows is a little lower than the 20 period EMA of the Closes [marker 1] but we have other mixed signals (see points 2, 3 & 4 below) to warn us away from this trade.

2) There is a clear pull-back of price to the 5 period EMA of the Lows, which would indicate a long trade.

3) The MACD has been above the zero line for some time but it is now in a strong overbought condition [marker 2] and the Stochastic on the 1-Hr chart is already dropping.

4) On the 15-minute chart, the Stochastic is almost in oversold territory [red arrow] but the Williams' %R and RSI are totally indecisive.

Hopefully you now understand what to look for and will not get fooled into opening positions when you should not but, just to be sure, we have prepared two more scenarios.

Classic example of when <u>not</u> to open a position.

In this case, we have an unwanted technical condition for a long position.

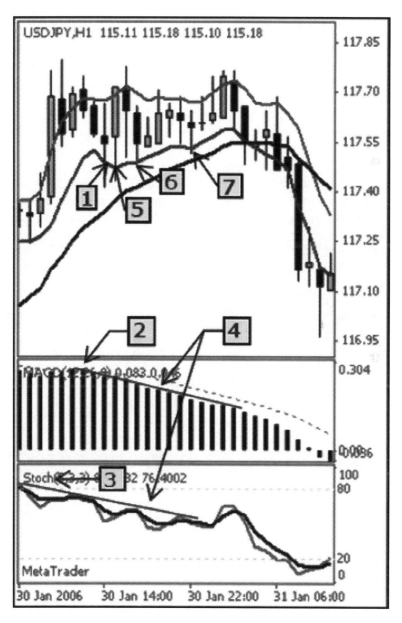

You can clearly see an opportunity to open a long position **[marker 1]**.

The MACD, however, is in an overbought state **[marker 2]** and the Stochastic is already moving out of and away from the overbought region **[marker 3]**.

In addition, the Stochastic is indicating the start of a bearish divergence **[marker 4]**.

Taking the entire situation into account, both the MACD and Stochastic are going down but the trend is still going up.

Under these conditions (**developing a bearish divergence**), every possible trade signal **[markers 5, 6, 7]** would be highly unlikely to achieve the target 25-30 pips required, meaning that any positions opened would almost certainly hit Stop Loss.

As with the entry rules for this strategy, the "walk away" rules for short positions are simply the reverse of the rules for long positions.

We now have one more example of technical conditions during which it is definitely not prudent to trade - **developing of a divergence.**

EUR/USD

Here we see very good opportunity to enter a short position.

The MACD is below the zero line and the downward movement of the MACD bars is just beginning.

But... you can see what has happened after that – **a bullish divergence on the Stochastic.**

If you open a position by accident and, shortly afterwards, you identify a divergence then close the trade without delay!

As you will have come to expect by now, bearish divergences are simply the reverse of bullish divergences like the one shown above i.e. the lines of the bearish divergence will be moving apart.

Please ensure you thoroughly reread the Trading Rules and Exit Strategies so that you understand how to identify the times when it is far better to stay out of the market. Your trading account will appreciate it!

By analyzing potential and actual trades, identifying when it is (or is not) safe to enter the market will become second nature to you.

Detailed Analysis of Trades

You may already have seen this chart on our web site.

Full set of trades

What we would like to do now is apply our technical indicators to the chart so that you can understand how all these trades have been identified.

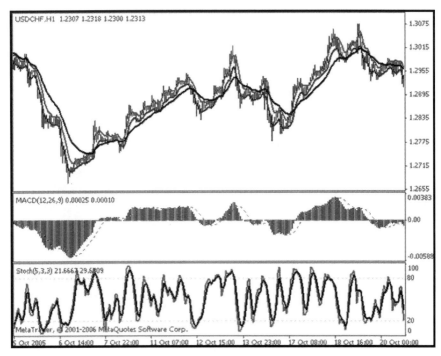

Non-informative chart

As you can see, in this state, our chart is not informative at all.

In order for us to see each trade, we need to zoom in on the chart and separate it into different sections.

> *Note: For analyzing these trades we will be using Exit Strategy №2. We would also like to remind to you that the 15-minute chart is only used to help us to enter and exit the market at more desirable price levels. In this section of the book we will not be using it at all to demonstrate how you can actually trade quite successfully without it.*

Finding trade opportunities

Ok! We have $1,000 to trade with and we can take any period of time. In our case, we will focus on the period from 2005-10-05 to 2005-10-20… 16 days.

To simplify things, <u>potential</u> trades (**not** guaranteed signals!) can be identified using our **Expert Advisor** plug-in for MetaTrader 4.

This small piece of software automatically monitors the market(s) and provides an audible alert when a potential trade opportunity presents itself, removing the need for you to be glued to the screen all day - you simply need to be within earshot of your computer to know when the right technical conditions have occurred.

You have already seen our first trade in the sections covering entry and exit rules for short positions so, to avoid needless repetition, we will start our analysis from the second trade.

Of course, to begin with, we need to calculate the profit from the first trade.

Trade 1 (1.2980-1.2744)

So, our first trade was opened at a price of 1.2980 and closed at a price of 1.2744. The profit was 236 pips.

The first position was closed by a Take Profit at 1.2949 which gave a 31 pip profit. However, that was 31 CHF which needs converting into USD as follows:

31 CHF / exchange rate of USD/CHF at close of trade (1.2949) = $24

The second position was closed at 1.2744 and gave a profit of 236 CHF.

236 CHF / exchange rate of UCD/CHF at close of trade (1.2744) = $185

$24 + $185 = $209 in total.

Ok! Time to examine Trade 2:

Trade 2 (1.2783-1.2903)

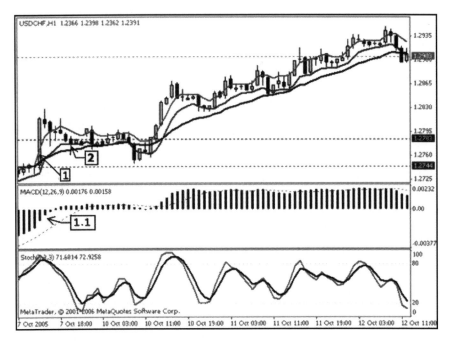

So, here we see our exit level (1.2744) for the second position of our first trade. The market is moving up but the MACD is remaining in negative territory **[markers 1, 1.1]** so we cannot go long until the MACD has at least three closed bars above the zero line.

After 7 hours, we finally got a trade alert from our Expert Advisor **[marker 2]**. We opened two 0.1 lot orders on the 4th bar of the MACD at a price of 1.2783.

Of course, for both orders we set the Stop Loss at 1.2738 and, for one, we set the Take Profit level at 1.2814. Unfortunately, price did not go up to the Take Profit level (1.2814) so our first order was not closed out. Moreover, price subsequently went down to 1.2748 but, happily, did not reach our Stop Loss level (1.2738).

Further strong up movement then developed. Our first order was closed at the Take Profit level of 1.2814 and so we moved the Stop Loss for the remaining order to our entry level (1.2783) while the market continued its uptrend.

Note that the MACD remains positive all the time and there are no price bars closing below the 20 period EMA of the Closes, meaning that we can safely maintain our position.

After forming the first low at 1.2824, we move our Stop Loss to 5 pips below this level (1.2819). This allows us to lock in our profit from the remaining order which has already achieved 91 pips.

By the way, note how many times during this uptrend that we could have entered other long positions. In practice, these would be opportunities to add to the existing position(s) after having locked in the earlier profits. Of course, this is just an observation - in this analysis we are not going to be adding to positions.

Finally, we encountered market conditions which met the rules of Exit Strategy 2 – a price bar has closed below the 20 period EMA of the Closes so we closed our position on the next price bar at a price of 1.2903 (120 pips).

Calculation

Our first order brought us 31 CHF ($24). (The calculation was covered previously when we looked at Trade 1).

Our second order brought us 120 CHF ($93), so the total profit for this trade was $117.

Adding this to the returns of our first trade gives us $326 profit.

Now, we all have different situations and responsibilities in our lives. It is just impossible to sit in front of a PC and trade twenty-four hours per day (as much as we may want to!) so, we will therefore cover two obvious scenarios:

a) when you are at your PC to monitor your trades and,

b) when you are not.

Ok! Now it is time to analyze Trade 3.

Trade 3 is going to be treated as though you were able to be at your PC to watch your trades.

Trade 3 (1.2870-1.2895) Lost Trade

We can see the exit level (1.2903) of the second order from our second trade. The market is continuing to go up but the MACD is remaining in negative territory **[markers 1, 1.1]**. Therefore, we cannot go long until the MACD moves above the zero line for at least three bars but, as we trade a two-way market, it means that it may be possible to go short.

After 7 hours, we got a trade alert from our Expert Advisor for opening a short position **[marker 2]**. We are going short on the 4th bar of the MACD with two 0.1 lot orders at an entry price of 1.2870. We see price clearly touch the 5 period EMA of the Highs. The MACD is remaining negative and the Stochastic looks good. We have all the right technical conditions for going short so we place a Take Profit on one order at 1.2839 and a Stop Loss on both orders at 1.2915.

Unfortunately, price went up and broke through the 5 period EMA of the Highs and the 20 period EMA of the Closes. This situation meets the rules of Exit Strategy №2 but we should really wait until the price bar <u>closes</u> above all three EMAs. As it closed at the

1.2900 level, we have little choice but to exit the trade without delay. The actual exit price is about 1.2895.

In this case we were not reliant on our Stop Losses to trigger because we rather quickly met the conditions of Exit Strategy 2.

Calculation

Our two orders made a combined loss of 50 CHF ($39).

> *Note: In this case we are assuming that you were at your PC and could act very quickly. If this were not so, the Stop Loss would still close the trade but at the higher price of 1.2915 and would lose 45 pips per order - $73 in total. We will need this sum in our final summary calculations.*

After our small defeat, we are now getting conditions for an impending trade alert to open a long position.

Time to take a look at Trade 4:

Trade 4 (1.2888-1.2975)

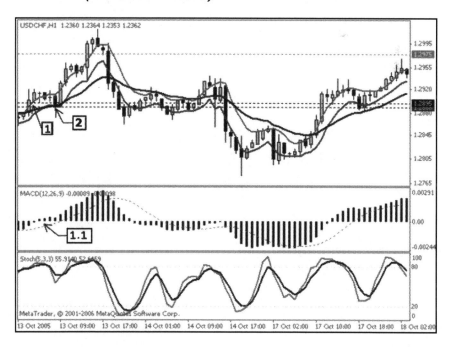

As usual, we can see our exit level (1.2895) from the previous trade marked with the black line. The market is going up and the MACD is going positive **[markers 1, 1.1]** but we cannot go long until we have at least 3 closed MACD bars above the zero line.

After 5 hours we get a trade alert from our Expert Advisor **[marker 2]** so we are going to open a long position on the 4th bar of the MACD – again, two 0.1 lot orders, at an entry price of 1.2888.

For both orders we are setting the Stop Loss at 1.2843 and, for one order, we are setting the Take Profit at 1.2919. Price goes up to the Take Profit level (1.2919) and the first order is closed.

Further strong upward movement developed and we moved the Stop Loss to our entry point (1.2888).

Calculation

Our first order brought us 31 CHF ($24) and the second order brought us 85 CHF ($65) = $89 in total.

Ok! Now time to start considering the next trade - Trade 5.

Trade 5 (1.2912-1.2881)

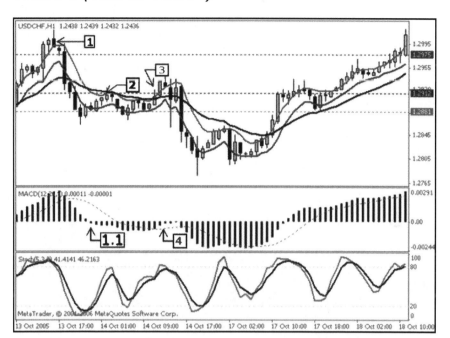

We see our exit level from the second order of the previous trade at 1.2975. The market has reversed and is going down. The MACD is going negative **[markers 1, 1.1]** but we still have to wait until we have our three negative MACD bars before going short.

It takes 10 hours but we eventually get a trade alert from our Expert Advisor **[marker 2]**. As before, we open a short position on the 4th bar of the MACD with two 0.1 lot orders. The entry price is 1.2912.

For both orders we place a Stop Loss at the 1.2957 level and for one of the orders we place our Take Profit at 1.2881. Price goes down to the 1.2868 level and our Take Profit closes the first order at 1.2881. We have banked our 31 CHF profit so we move the Stop Loss for the second order the entry point level (1.2912).

Unfortunately, price starts going back up, and our remaining order is closed by the Stop Loss at a price of 1.2912 **[marker 3]**.

Further minimal upward movement developed but the MACD remained negative **[marker 4]** which means we can wait for another opportunity to open a short position.

Calculation

The first order earned us 31 CHF ($24) and the second order broke even so the total profit from this trade was $24.

Now, on to Trade 6:

Trade 6 (1.2846-1.2815)

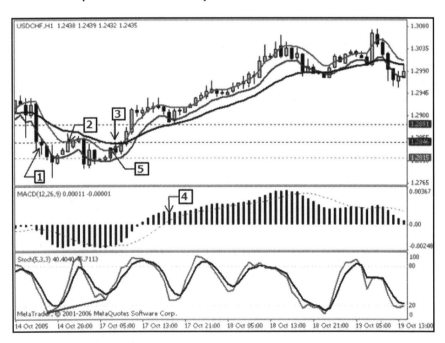

Trade 6 followed almost the same pattern as Trade 5.

We see our exit level (1.2881) from the previous short trade. The market is continuing down and the MACD is staying in the negative zone **[marker 1]**. We now just need to wait until price touches the 5 period EMA of the Highs.

It took 20 hours but we got a trade alert from our Expert Advisor **[marker 2]** so we opened a short position with two 0.1 lot orders. The price achieved is 1.2846.

Our Stop Loss level for both orders was 1.2891 and the Take Profit level for one order was set at 1.2815. Price goes down to 1.2794 and the Take Profit was hit, closing the first order at 1.2815. This gave us 31 CHF profit. We also moved the Stop Loss for the second order to the entry level (1.2846).

Regrettably, price goes back up, and our remaining order is closed by the Stop Loss at break-even (1.2846) **[marker 3]**.

Further strong upward movement developed and the MACD moves into the positive zone **[marker 4]** which means we have to wait for an opportunity to open a long position.

> **Note:** After Trade 6 we could potentially open one more short position [marker 5] but, according our No Trade Rules (which you should remember), such a position would have been unjustified and therefore more likely to result in a loss.

Calculation

Our first order has made 31 CHF ($24) and our second order simply broke even as it was closed by our Stop Loss. Trade 6 therefore made $24 in total.

Time to look at our final trade:

Trade 7 (1.2891-1.2990)

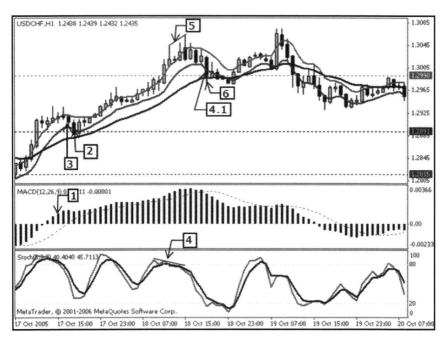

Trade 7 has ideal technical conditions for going long.

We see our exit level from the previous short trade at 1.2815, the market is moving upwards and the MACD is remaining in the positive zone **[marker 1]**. Now we simply need to wait until price touches the 5 period EMA of the Lows.

It takes 20 hours but we finally got a trade signal from our Expert Advisor **[marker 2]** and so we open a long position with two 0.1 lot orders. The entry price is 1.2891.

Our Stop Loss for both orders is set at 1.2846 and our Take Profit for one order is set at 1.2922. Price goes up without stopping and the Take Profit closes our first order at 1.2922 giving us our normal 31 CHF profit. We then move the Stop Loss for the second order to the break-even point (1.2891).

Strong upward movement developed and the MACD remains in the positive zone. Moreover, price remains higher than both the 5 period EMA of the Lows and the 20 period EMA of the Closes

[marker 3] which means we want to hold this position as long as possible and hope that the rules of our Exit Strategy are not met for a very long time!

As you can see, the rules of Exit Strategies 3 and 2 were met one after the other **[markers 4, 4.1]**.

It is actually more advantageous for us to exit using Strategy 3 **[marker 5]** but, as we decided to use Strategy 2 in this "walk-thru", that is what we will do so, we close our remaining order using Exit Strategy 2 after a price bar closes below the 20 period EMA of the Closes **[marker 6]**.

Calculation

The first order brought us 31 CHF ($24) and the second order brought us 99 CHF ($76) = $100 in total.

At this point we will finish covering the **MAIN FOREX SYSTEM –** "Day-Trading".

Calculation of profit from all 7 trades

1) If we were monitoring Trade 3

> Trade 1: $209
> Trade 2: $117
> Trade 3: -$39
> Trade 4: $89
> Trade 5: $24
> Trade 6: $24
> Trade 7: $100

Total from 2005-10-05 to 2005-10-18 (14 days) = $524

That equates to more than 50% profit in 14 days, or 1,303% per annum.

2) If we were <u>not</u> monitoring Trade 3

> Trade 1: $209
> Trade 2: $117
> Trade 3: -$73
> Trade 4: $89
> Trade 5: $24
> Trade 6: $24
> Trade 7: $100

Total from 2005-10-05 to 2005-10-18 (14 days) = $490

That is still 49% profit in 14 days, or 1,277% per annum.

Illustrated Trades for 2011:

As we already know how the Main FOREX System works, we will now review some fresh trades - both with and without filtering indicators.

Combined Example EUR/USD

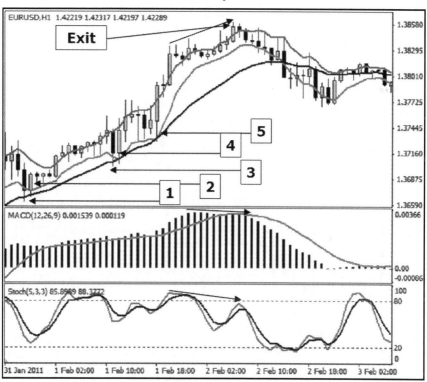

5 Long Trades

EUR/USD

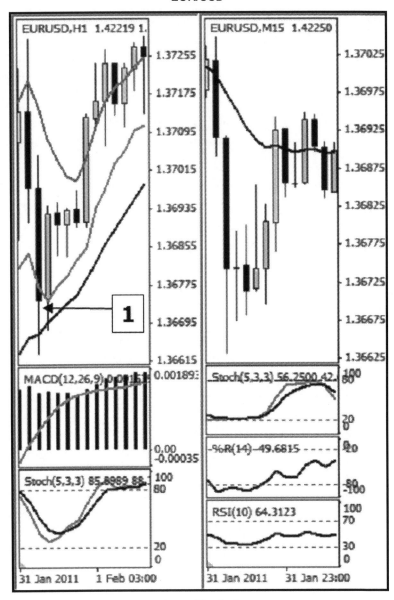

Long Trade 1

EUR/USD

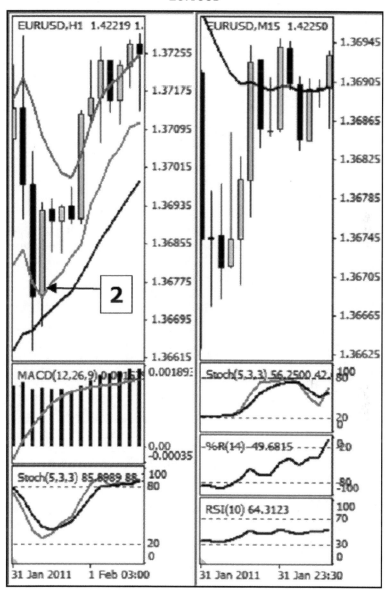

Long Trade 2

Using the rules of Exit Strategy №3 (Using Divergences)

Trade 1 - Hypothetical profit is 179 (204) pips in 32 hours

Trade 2 - Hypothetical profit is 179 (204) pips in 31 hours

We have equal profit (in pips) for both trades as our entry and exit levels are identical in each case – the only difference is a 1 hour variation in the entry price bar. It would certainly have been possible to catch either of the trade entries and ridden the trend until the divergence-based exit signal [Exit] on the main chart above. Our standard approach of opening two orders and closing one at 25 pips profit while riding the other until the divergence exit signal occurred, would have achieved 179 + 25 = 204 pips. Of course, the actual cash profit achieved would depend upon the size of your initial positions.

To save time, we will not illustrate each of the remaining entry points – instead, we will just summarize the profit potential of entering those trades.

Trade 3 - Hypothetical profit is 140 (165) pips in 19 hours

Trade 4 - Hypothetical profit is 138 (163) pips in 19 hours

Trade 5 - Hypothetical profit is 118 (143) pips in 12 hours

Brief description of the two long positions illustrated above:

Trade 1 (EUR/USD)

1) The 5 period EMA of the Lows is above the 20 period EMA of the Closes – a strong confirmation!

2) There is a clear pull-back of price to the 5 period EMA of the Lows.

3) The MACD is above the zero line and looks to be moving further upward and the Stochastic is in middle-ground.

4) On the 15-minute chart, Stochastic, Williams' %R and RSI are all indicating an oversold condition.

Trade 2 (EUR/USD)

1) The 5 period EMA of the Lows is above the 20 period EMA of the Closes – a strong confirmation!

2) There is a clear pull-back of price to the 5 period EMA of the Lows.

3) The MACD is above the zero line and the Stochastic is in upper-ground.

4) On the 15-minute chart, Stochastic, Williams' %R and RSI are all indicating an oversold condition.

Combined Example EUR/USD

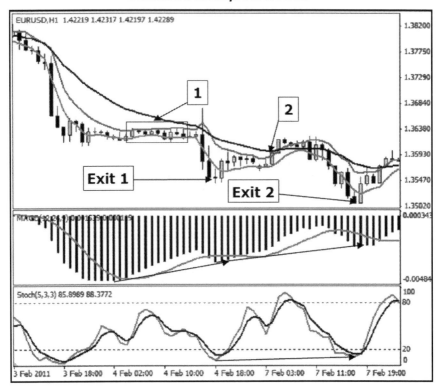

2 Short Groups of Trades

Marker 1 indicates the location of 6 trade opportunities within a few bars and Marker 2 indicates the location of an additional 2 potential trades.

All of the trade opportunities indicated by Marker 1 have almost identical entry levels and any one of them traded through to the divergence-based exit signal [Exit 2] at 1.35050 would have achieved 135 pips profit. The initial Exit signal [Exit 1] was actually slightly vague but would still have resulted in 89 pips profit had you decided to use it.

EUR/USD

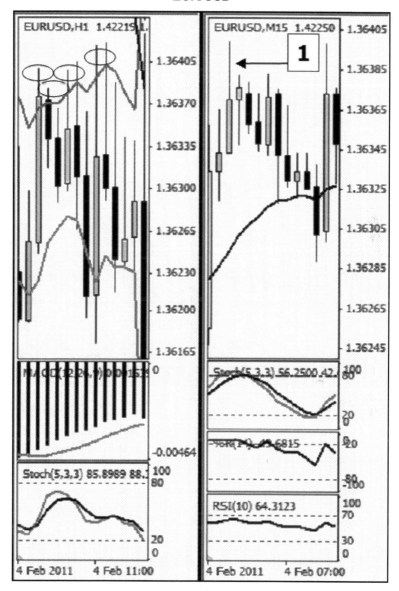

All 6 Trades

[Marker 1] on the chart above shows where the first of 6 possible trade entries occurred (marked by the 4 ovals).

EUR/USD

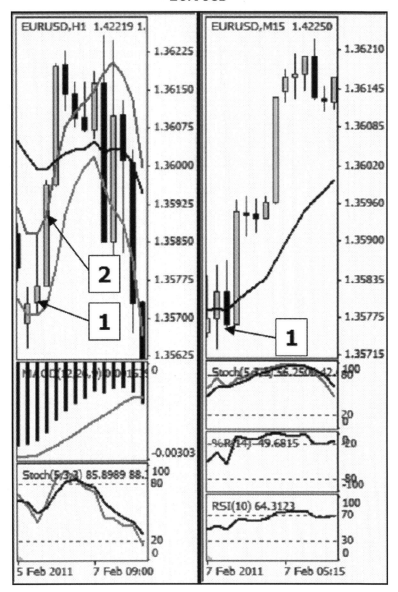

2 Short Trades

On the chart above, **[Marker 1]** and **[Marker 2]** show the two additional trade opportunities which occurred after Exit point 1.

An interesting EUR/USD example

7 additional opportunities to open a position!

You already know how the system works, so it should now be easy for you to find trade opportunities on your own.

Long and Short USD/CHF positions

USD/CHF

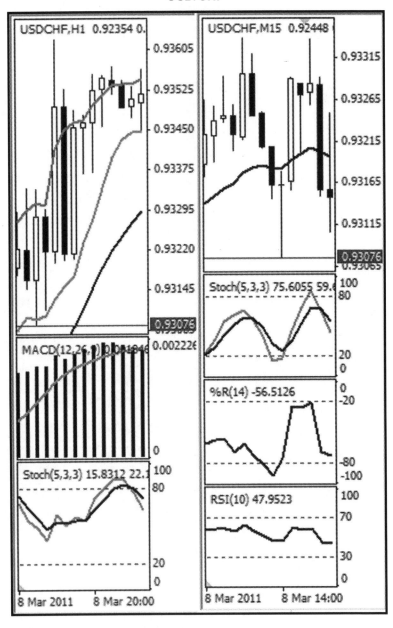

One potential long trade

USD/CHF

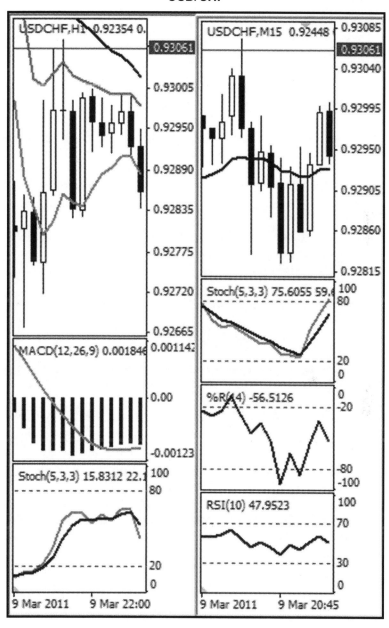

Two potential short trades (treated as just 1 trade)

Brief description of the two positions illustrated above:

Trade 1 – Long (USD/CHF)

1) The 5 period EMA of the Lows is above the 20 period EMA of the Closes – a strong confirmation!

2) There is a clear pull-back of price to the 5 period EMA of the Lows.

3) The MACD is above the zero line and looks to be moving further upward and the Stochastic is in middle-ground.

4) On the 15-minute chart, Stochastic and Williams' %R are both indicating an oversold condition. RSI is indicating a middle condition.

Trade 2 – Short (USD/CHF)

1) The 5 period EMA of the Highs is above the 20 period EMA of the Closes – a strong confirmation!

2) There is a clear pull-back of price to the 5 period EMA of the Highs.

3) The MACD is below the zero line and the Stochastic is in upper-ground.

4) On the 15-minute chart, Stochastic and RSI are both indicating a middle condition. – still okay for us. Williams' %R is indicating an oversold condition.

Long and short USD/JPY positions

USD/JPY

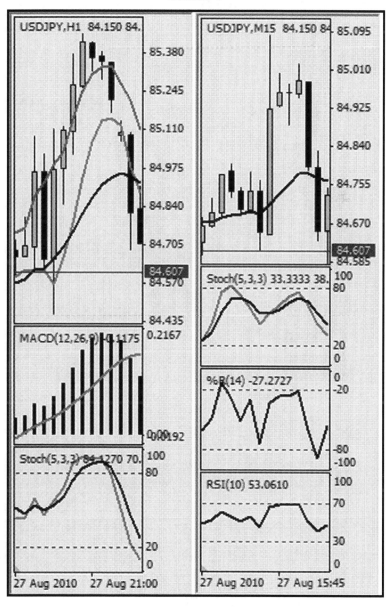

One potential long trade

USD/JPY

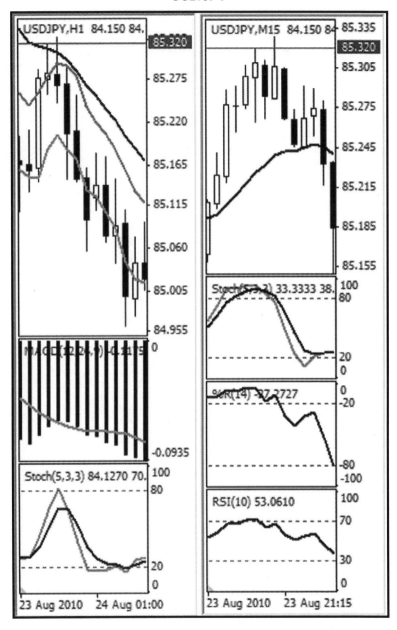

Two potential short trades (treated as just one trade)

Brief description of the two positions illustrated above:

Trade 1 – Long (USD/JPY)

1)   The 5 period EMA of the Lows is a little above the 20 period EMA of the Closes – a strong confirmation!

2)   There is a clear pull-back of price to the 5 period EMA of the Lows.

3)   The MACD is above the zero line and looks to be moving further upward and the Stochastic is in middle-ground.

4)   On the 15-minute chart, Stochastic is indicating an oversold condition, Williams' %R and RSI are all indicating a middle condition – still okay for us.

Trade 2 – Short (USD/JPY)

1)   The 5 period EMA of the Lows is above the 20 period EMA of the Closes – a strong confirmation!

2)   There is a clear pull-back of price to the 5 period EMA of the Lows.

3)   The MACD is above the zero line and the Stochastic is in upper-ground.

4)   On the 15-minute chart, Stochastic, Williams' %R and RSI are all indicating an oversold condition.

Long and short GBP/USD positions

GBP/USD

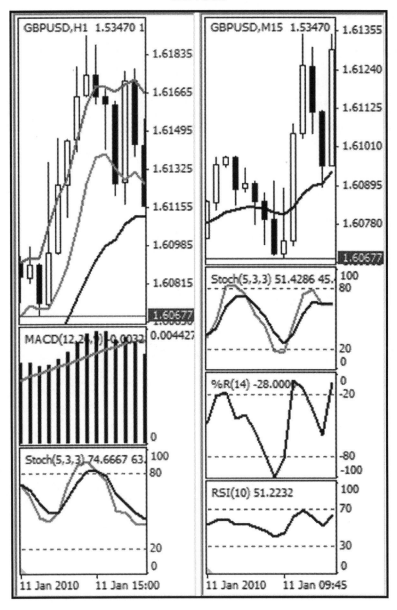

Two potential long trades (treated as just 1 trade)

GBP/USD

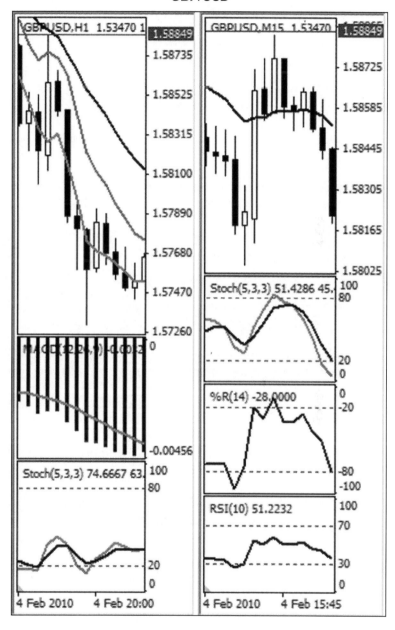

One potential short trade

Brief description of the two positions illustrated above:

Trade 1 – Long (GBP/USD)

1) The 5 period EMA of the Lows is above the 20 period EMA of the Closes – a strong confirmation!

2) There is a clear pull-back of price to the 5 period EMA of the Lows.

3) The MACD is above the zero line and looks to be moving further upward and the Stochastic is in middle-ground.

4) On the 15-minute chart, Stochastic, Williams' %R and RSI are all indicating an oversold condition.

Trade 2 – Short (GBP/USD)

1) The 5 period EMA of the Lows is above the 20 period EMA of the Closes – a strong confirmation!

2) There is a clear pull-back of price to the 5 period EMA of the Lows.

3) The MACD is above the zero line and the Stochastic is in upper-ground.

4) On the 15-minute chart, Stochastic and Williams' %R are both indicating an oversold condition and only RSI is in middle-ground.

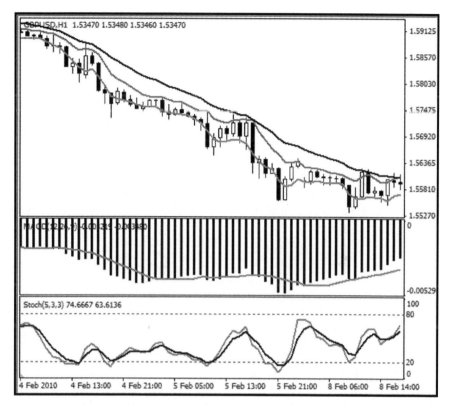

Series of short trades between the 4th and 8th of February

Look how many short trades you could have taken between the 4th and 8th of February.

In the chart section above, you can see that trade opportunities are occurring all of the time and very frequently occur one after the other.

A few words about the 45 pip Stop Loss

Loss failure

In the image above, you can see that our 45 pip Stop Loss is quite resilient – the large price spike is actually just 35.5 pips so was not pronounced enough to trigger the Stop Loss of the position opened at 1.36401 (marked by the line and down-arrow). This is a great example of a Stop Loss that is not too small and not too large either.

Please also notice how many entry points there are around the 1.3640 level and many more possible entry points would come into view if you scrolled the chart to the right.

About filters

We mentioned earlier that we would discuss trading with and without filters but we first need to clarify is what we actually mean by a filter.

A common misconception is that the 15-minute chart is a filter for this trading system but nothing could be further from the truth. The 15-minute chart simply provides a set of indicators that we can use to find a better entry level for our trades.

In fact, the **only** filter we use is the 20 period EMA of the Close.

The following chart illustrates the point...

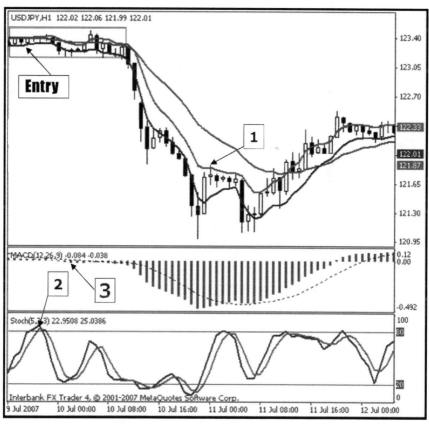

Trading With / Without A Filter

If using the 20 period EMA of the Closes, we have only one clear trade opportunity, indicated by **[marker 1]**.

However, if you look at the top-left of the chart (marked by the rectangle), there are several trade opportunities – we simply would not have taken them because our filter condition was not met but, by discounting the filter, we could have entered a trade much earlier.

Why would it have been possible to enter a trade at that time?

Because the MACD is below the zero line (indicated by **[marker 3]**) and the Stochastic is in overbought territory but moving out of that zone as indicated by **[marker 2]**.

Ultimately, use of the filter is your decision – if you use the filter then you will have fewer trade opportunities but those trades will be more accurate and better confirmed.

"To filter, or not to filter" really just depends on your trading style - if you are an active and more risk-tolerant trader then you will get more opportunities to trade by discounting the filter but, if you are more of a conservative trader then you should probably make use of the filter and accept fewer, more accurate trade entries.

Conclusion for the Main FOREX SYSTEM – "Day-Trading"

We think you will grow to like this system more and more as you spend more time trading it. From our perspective, we have tried our best to explain how to trade this system and we have tried to illustrate trades in as much detail as possible. That leaves you at the point where you really just need to gain first-hand experience to build up your confidence in this 1st part of the strategy.

Now we want to introduce you to the second part of this trading system: something that you can use in concert with the Day-Trading system we already covered to gain additional profits.

CHAPTER 11
TRADING RULES FOR THE MAIN
FOREX SYSTEM-"Scalping"

Introduction

The Main Scalping systems are intended to help you gain small, additional profits during trading that boost your gains from the main "Day Trading" system.

So, what does it all mean?

Basically that you can open additional positions once your second order is already in profit and the Stop Loss level for it has been moved to break-even.

Your objective here is to enter and exit the market with the aim of catching 5-15 pips in addition to any existing and/or anticipated profits from the main trade.

So, let us begin…

Main Rules

Scalping the trend of the 60-minute timeframe.

Enter additional positions using bounces off the 20 period EMA of the Closes on the 15-minute chart. Though not totally necessary, it is always good to have confirmation from the overbought/oversold condition of the technical indicators on the 15-minute chart.

Exiting these additional positions is by mandatory confirmation from the overbought/oversold conditions of the technical indicators on the 15-minute chart.

USD/JPY

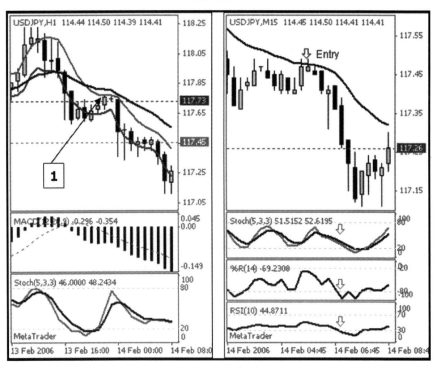

Short Position

Assume that we opened a short position at 117.73 using the Day-Trading system. The Take Profit closed one order at 117.45 and we moved the Stop Loss level down to the entry price of 117.73 for the remaining order.

Our remaining order is now protected from loss by the Stop Loss and we can try to catch some additional profits without concerning ourselves with losses.

Price is below both our 5 period EMAs and, importantly, the 5 period EMA of the Highs is below the 20 period EMA of the Closes **[marker 1]**. These are ideal conditions to scalp extra profits.

On the 15-minute chart, price bounced from the 20 period EMA of the Closes so we opened an additional 0.1 lot order at 117.43.

Though the Stochastic was still in our favor, the Williams' %R and RSI began showing an oversold condition (red arrows on the 15-minute chart), so it was time to close our scalp trade at the 117.26 level (the dotted line on the 15-minute chart above).

In this instance, we managed to grab an additional 17 pips - a very good result!

USD/JPY

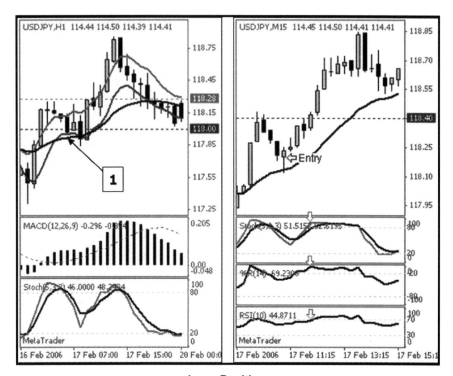

Long Position

Here, we opened a long position at 118.00 using the Day-Trading system. The Take Profit closed one order at 118.28 and we moved the Stop Loss for the remaining order to the break-even point (118.00).

Our remaining order is fully protected from loss so we can try to catch some additional profit.

Price is higher than both of our 5 period EMAs and, as a bonus, the 5 period EMA of the Lows is higher than the 20 period EMA of the Closes **[marker 1]**. Again, ideal conditions to scalp some additional profits.

On the 15-minute chart, price drops back down and bounces off the 20 period EMA of the Closes so we open an additional position at a price of 118.20.

Because all indicators show an overbought condition (red arrows on the 15-minute chart), we close our trade at a price of 118.40 (dotted line on the 15-minute chart above).

An additional 20 pips – another fine trade!

Conclusion

We covered the main trading rules for the Scalping System so now let us consider some additional methods which you can use for scalping profits.

An alternative way to scalp profits

As the end of this book is approaching, we thought we would just highlight another reason why you will want to study the **Essential Fibonacci and Divergence Strategies** once it is available – yes, we know we keep reminding you but it is an important approach to master.

Anyway, here are a couple of illustrated examples of divergences being used when scalping:

Divergence on 15-minute chart

USD/JPY

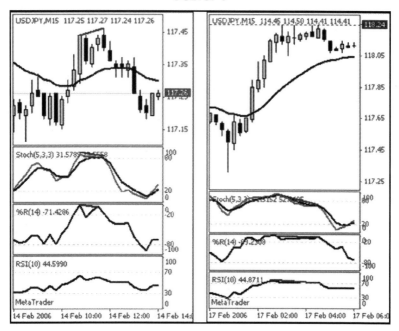

Short Position

As you can see, the left-hand chart shows a clear bearish divergence between price and the Stochastic indicator which would be our cue to enter a quick short scalp or exit a long trade.

USD/JPY

Long Position

Here, the left-hand chart shows a clear bullish divergence between price and each of the three indicators. This very pronounced divergence would prompt us to enter a quick long scalp or exit a short trade immediately.

Conclusion for Main FOREX SYSTEM – "Scalping"

At this point we would like to wrap up this section on scalping.

You will encounter many opportunities to make use of the two methods we have shown you. They are just two of many scalping techniques but, it is far more important that you become proficient in one or two methods and actually make money from them, than to know 50 methods that you never use!

Evolved FOREX Trading

PART II

PREFACE TO PART II

Many clients have repeatedly asked us two specific questions:

- Can the strategy be improved to get more trades?

- Can the strategy be adapted to the daily chart timeframe?

In fact, although the system was been developed to work optimally using 60 minute charts, it can also be used very effectively with daily charts - this is a great bonus for traders who are unable to monitor the markets during the day.

In this "Advanced" module, we cover additional methods of using the Main FOREX System. It includes using the system on a daily basis and also using other technical indicators with the basic strategy.

Understanding the rules:

The advanced methods outlined within this section are based on, and build upon, the prime strategy rules of the Main FOREX System which are explained earlier in this book. Please ensure that you have read and understand the rules of the standard strategy before moving to these advanced methods.

Summary of indicators and their settings:

1-Hour Chart

- 5 period EMA of the Highs
- 5 period EMA of the Lows
- 20 period EMA of the Closes
- Stochastic (5,3,3) **or** 5EMAs Advanced (24)
- MACD (12,26,9)

Daily Chart

- 5 period EMA of the Highs
- 5 period EMA of the Lows
- 20 period EMA of the Closes
- Stochastic (5,3,3)
- MACD (12,26,9)

CHAPTER 1
ADVANCED METHOD 1
Breakout System

This method relies on the use of Support & Resistance lines together with the standard Main strategy method. You therefore need to identify a range, with its highest and lowest levels, to trade the breakouts in addition to trading the pullbacks.

It is important to realize that the EvolvedAlert EA determines the trend by following the standard rules of the Main FOREX System i.e. it uses principally EMAs and MACD. If, however, you apply lines of Support & Resistance then you will gain several advantages. Let us see what they are:

1. You will be able to determine the existence of flat market conditions. The standard Main FOREX System is not designed to work in these situations so you can avoid losing trades by switching to a strategy designed for flat market conditions.

2. You will be able to use the Main system as a Moving Average cross-over system, however, only in terms of providing additional trade confirmations in our case.

3. The standard Main FOREX System is a trend following system designed for trading pullbacks, but now you can trade breakouts too.

Look at the chart on the next page for an example:

Clear trade signal

As you can see from the chart above, there is quite a good move from about 123.16 down to about 121.26.

If you were using the standard Main FOREX System rules then you would only get a signal at the 121.86 level and could trade it down to about 121.08. The result: just 78 pips. In other words, you missed out on the movement from 123.16 down to 121.86. This equates to 123 pips of lost opportunity & potential profit!

But how could we have gained a greater trading opportunity from this scenario?

By approaching the market like this:

Previous price range

Notice the horizontal lines at 123.51 and 123.16 – these indicate the previous price range.

When the market has been ranging after a reasonable sized move, it indicates that volatility is reducing and a breakout is possible in the near future.

As you can see from the chart, the breakout happened in a downward direction. We therefore require trading rules which allow us to capitalize on this type of scenario which, fortunately, we have!

Breakout Rules

Breakout Rule 1

We need to determine the highest and lowest levels of a range so we need at least one extreme point for each level and, for drawing lines of Support & Resistance, we need at least two points for each of the range boundaries.

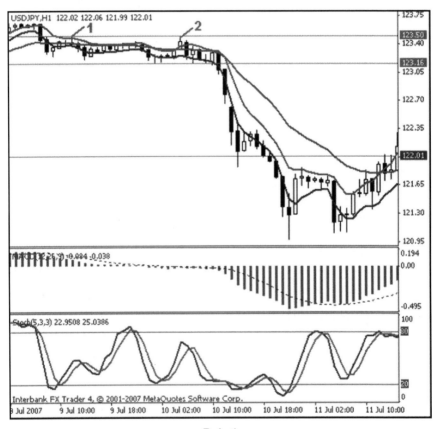

Rule 1

Point 1 is at 123.50 and point two is at 123.48. By drawing a line at the 123.50 level (the higher of the two), we have determined the upper boundary of the range.

We now need to determine the lower boundary so look at the following chart:

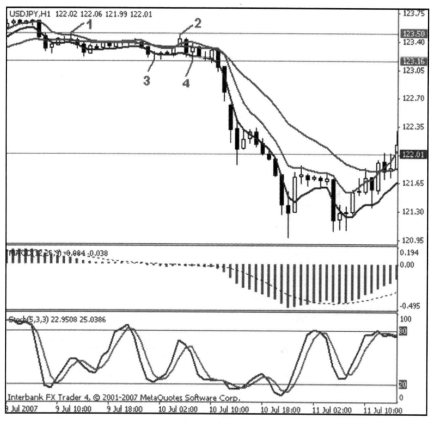

The lower boundary

Point 3 is at 123.17 and point 4 is at 123.16. We use the 123.16 level accordingly, being the lower of the two, and draw a trend line.

Stop Orders:

There are many methods for trading breakouts; the most widely used approach is to place Stop orders 3-5 pips above and below the defined range boundaries, however, we have our own approach.

Breakout Rule 2

We need to wait until a "1 hour" price bar closes above the Resistance level for a long position or below the Support level for a short position.

Rule 2

Breakout Rule 3

For a long position, the 5 period EMA of the Lows must have crossed the 20 period EMA of the Closes from below to above and, for a short position, the 5 period EMA of the Highs must have crossed the 20 period EMA of the Closes from above to below.

Rule 3

Breakout Rule 4

For a long position, the MACD must be in the positive zone (above zero) and for a short position, in the negative zone (below zero).

That covers all the conditions for the first part of the Main FOREX System Breakouts Trading strategy.

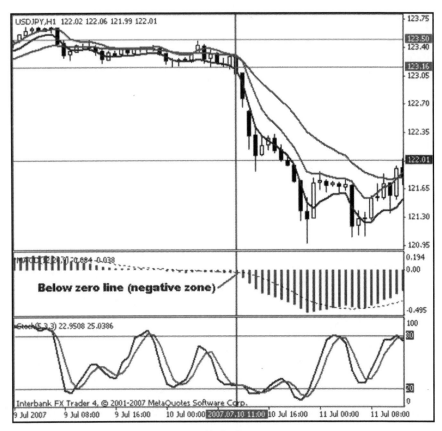

Rule 4

As you should have noticed, we covered trading rules for both long and short positions in the first part of this strategy description.

Now, we can continue with the second part of the strategy - for a short position in this example.

Suppose that you missed the first trade signal, the breakout at 123.16 (it is impossible to be awake and ready to trade all of the time!) so you want to trade the next opportunity. How do we identify it? For this we have some tools!

Please note: As long as price remains below both the 5 period EMA of the Highs and the 20 period EMA of the Closes, we can go short – conditions would simply need to be reversed (using the 5 period EMA of the Lows) when looking at a long position.

Short trade possibilities

The zone for short trade possibilities is shown by the rectangle which is drawn from the 123.16 breakout level across to the price bar indicated by the comment "First up-close above two EMAs".

That particular price bar also indicates an exit point based on one of the "exit strategies" in the standard Main FOREX System course.

So, what additional trade(s) can we find, having missed the first one? Well, look at the next chart:

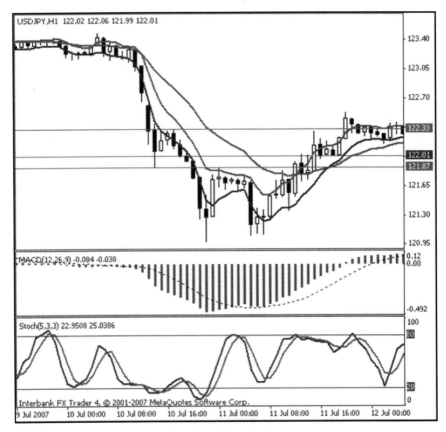

A pullback beginning

Within the zone of the rectangle (shorting possibilities) on the previous chart we have a pullback beginning at 121.87 and ending at 122.33 which has been marked with horizontal lines.

The line at 121.87 is indicating both the end of the pullback and another breakout level. However, the pullback did not create a trade signal using the standard Main FOREX System trading rules.

You are probably wondering: "How do I predict the beginning and end of a pullback?" Well, you simply use the proprietary method we have developed and that will be revealed next. Take special note of it as you will not find it in **any** other course.

As can be seen on the previous chart:

1. The pullback did not extend beyond either the 5 period EMA of the Highs or the 20 period EMA of the Closes – actually, not even the 5 period EMA of the Lows was totally breached, just overlaid.

2. During the pullback, the MACD remained negative.

These points indicated a failed pullback with the possibility of a second breakout to the downside (the current main trend direction in this case).

To clarify, the market moved up after a strong downward movement creating the first white (bullish) price bar – it indicates the beginning of the pullback.

After that, a second white (bullish) price bar was formed, followed by a black (bearish) price bar.

All this occurred while price remained below both the 5 period EMA of the Highs and the 20 period EMA of the Closes and the MACD was in the negative zone throughout, as shown on the following chart:

All trade activities

If you look at the following chart, you will see where (when the move was almost over) a clear trade entry signal was finally generated using the rules of standard Main FOREX System:

Standard signal

The best possible trade that could have been obtained from the standard signal was from 121.86 down to about 121.08 – a move of 78 pips.

Conclusion for Advanced Method 1

If using only the standard Main FOREX System strategy we would have identified just one signal and gained a maximum of 78 pips. By using Advanced Method 1, the entire move from the initial breakout level of 123.16 down to 121.08 was possible – potentially, 208 pips.

So far, we have covered a short (SELL) position. Now let us look at an example of a long (BUY) position.

Upward breakout

Look at the chart above. All conditions have been met; but in this case, for a long position. The Support & Resistance lines indicate the range as being between 1.3594 and 1.3642, which has finally been broken by the price bar indicated (the line at 1.3654 indicates the breakout level). Also we see crossover of the 5 period EMA of the Lows and the 20 period EMA of the Closes from below in addition to the positive condition of the MACD.

Following this, we can see two pullbacks which resulted in breakouts in the direction of the original upward breakout and new main trend.

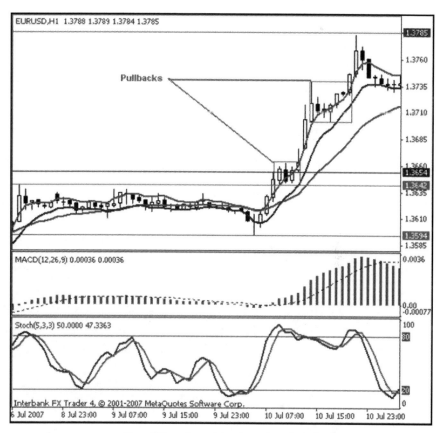

Possibly missed trade entry signal

From the example above, it is blatantly obvious that by using just the standard Main FOREX System trading rules, we would not have identified a single trade entry signal during the entire upward move. That is why the advanced method was introduced.

CHAPTER 2
ADVANCED METHOD 2
Main Standard System
On A Daily Basis "A"

This method is actually very simple. You just need to lengthen the timeframe.

Whereas the standard Main FOREX System uses the 60 minute and 15 minute timeframes, here we need to use the Daily and 60 minute timeframes instead.

Of course, this approach results in a slight "problem": a longer timeframe requires a correspondingly larger Stop Loss.

Can you allow yourself, and do you even want, to use a 130-200 pip Stop Loss when trading? This is a question that only you can answer.

Standard Main System on a Daily Basis can be used only to determine the trend direction. There is one specific exception to the standard criteria: you do not need to use the "3+ MACD bars" rule for this method, the MACD simply needs to be positive for a long position and negative for a short position.

One other point to bear in mind - the normal "exit strategies" defined in the standard **Main FOREX System** are unsuitable for trading on a daily timeframe. It is far better to use Support & Resistance levels to indicate points to exit trades.

That said; let us see what we can do. For this, we need to look at the next chart:

Many wonderful trades

Just look at the chart and see how many wonderful trades you could have made by using the **Standard Main System on a Daily Basis** method.

Let us define zones for both long and short positions...

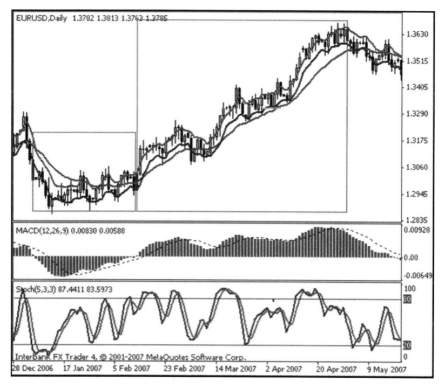

Positions zones

The small rectangle (on the left) shows the "short positions" zone.

The large rectangle (on the right) shows the "long positions" zone.

There is no need to reiterate the standard strategy rules, simply remember the differences:

- No "3+ MACD bars" rule.

- Support & Resistance levels replace the standard exit strategies.

On a Daily chart, Support & Resistance levels are usually the Low and High of the previous day.

For instance, if a trade signal occurred on 10th June, Support & Resistance levels for that day would be the Low and High of 9th June.

A short position example:

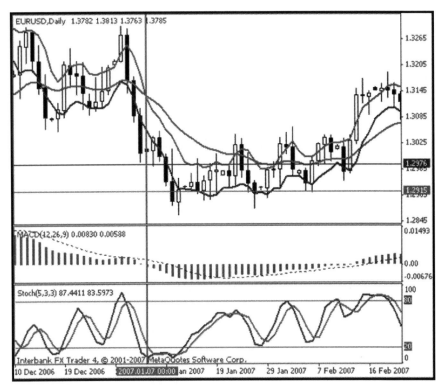

The first short position

Look at the chart above.

The first trade signal (short position) occurred on 2007.01.16, marked by the horizontal line at 1.2976.

As a target, we should use the Low of the previous day – 2007.01.15 - marked by the red horizontal line at 1.2915.

CHAPTER 3
ADVANCED METHOD 2.
Main Standard System
On A Daily Basis "B"

Method 2 (basis "B") involves using both the 5 period EMAs of the Lows and Highs to indicate the range for intraday trades.

Trading Rules:

1. The MACD should be positive for a long position and negative for a short position, as for all Main methods.

2. Before going short, price should touch the 5EMA of the Highs. Before going long, price should touch the 5EMA of the Low.

That is simple enough, so let us examine a couple of examples, beginning with the first trade signal of our buying zone closest to the current date.

The goal of this process is to prove that such trade opportunities occur all of the time.

Time to look at the next chart:

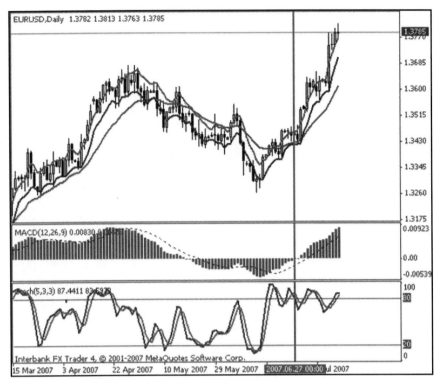

The buying zone

The buying zone is to the right of the vertical line (dated 2007.06.27).

The first trade signal we encounter is on 2007.07.10. Let us magnify the chart to see things more clearly:

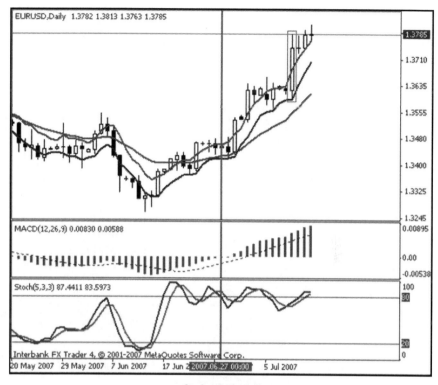

A clear signal

We could have used the first price bar after the vertical line and, in fact, the next price bar too, but these were not clear signals.

The price bar dated 2007.07.10 and marked with a rectangle on the chart, however, is a very clear signal for going long.

Ok! Let us locate this day on the 60 minute chart:

Retrace then move back upwards

On that day, the market opened at 1.3620 (marked by the middle horizontal line) then came down to 1.3594, which coincides with the 5EMA of the Lows on the Daily chart, after which it retraced and moved back upwards.

The range from 1.3594 to 1.3784 can be used as the trading range for intraday trading on that day – it would be perfect, but remember what we discussed at the beginning of this section... to use both of the 5EMAs (of the Highs and Lows) to indicate the trading range. That would make the range boundaries 1.3594 and 1.3675 (81 pips, not counting the spread) as shown on the following chart.

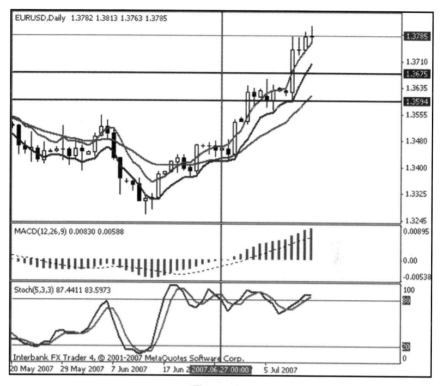

The range

The range mentioned is indicated by the horizontal lines on the chart above.

That is all. By being familiar with the main rules of the standard Main FOREX System, you will understand how to apply and use these methods very quickly.

Now let us examine an example of how we can combine the Main FOREX System with other technical indicators or even with custom (non-standard) technical indicators.

In the next section, we are not going to examine lots of technical indicators – instead, we will concentrate on just one to illustrate the point.

CHAPTER 4
ADVANCED METHOD 3
Main System - Standard And
Custom Indicators

In this section we are going to introduce a custom indicator – the 5EMAs Advanced indicator, which will be used in place of the more usual Stochastic indicator. Again, when using this method, we do not need to adhere to the standard "3+ bars of MACD" rule.

The goal of this section is not specifically to show how the Main FOREX System works with other indicators – more to demonstrate that complete trading systems can be successfully combined with other indicators and/or Expert Advisors to further enhance the quality of entry signals.

Experimentation is the key to success!

If you have not already done so, please install the 5EMAs Advanced indicator using the auto-installer available from the member area of the **www.EvolvedForexTrading.com** website.

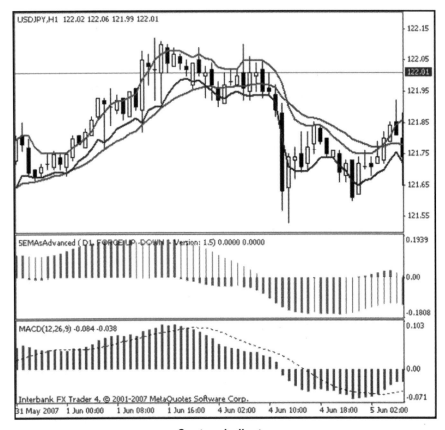

Custom indicator

The trading rules are very straightforward.

Using the rules of the Main FOREX System, only:

- enter *long* positions when the up bars (above zero line) of the 5EMAs Advanced indicator are solid (thick).

- enter *short* positions when the down bars (below zero line) of the 5EMAs Advanced indicator are solid (thick).

As previously explained, we do not require the Stochastic indicator in this case, but we still need the MACD to be in the positive zone for long positions and in the negative zone for short positions.

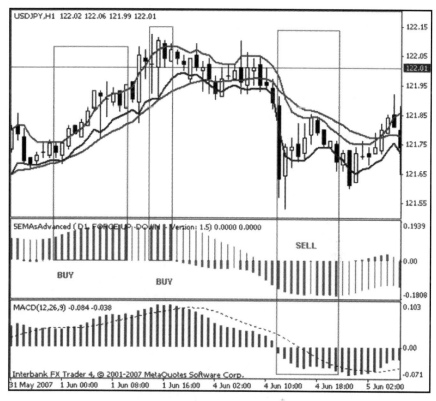

Buy and Sell zones

On the chart above we have marked the BUY opportunity zones with rectangles (left-hand) and a SELL opportunity zone with a rectangle (right-hand).

This indicator can serve as great filter for avoiding false entries that are sometimes generated by the standard trading rules and indicators of the Main FOREX System.

We hope you take time to master these standard and advanced methods and wish you great success in your trading career.

> ***Note***: *All images in this book have been made using MT4 from various brokers. This was done specially to show that these systems work with any all MT4 brokers.*

APPENDIX

Trading Plans

Conservative Traders

1) Aim to risk 10% of your account equity.

For example, if available equity was $1,000:

- open a 0.20 lot position as 2 x 0.10 lot orders

- set a 25 pip TP on one order and a 45-60 pip SL on both.

  Note:

  Due to the current, very unstable market conditions, we recommend using a 60 pip SL rather than the more usual 45 pips, depending on observed market volatility.

2) When the market has moved 25 pips into profit:

- half of your position closes automatically, leaving the other half running

- **do not** adjust the SL level of the remaining order

3) When market has moved a further 25 pips into profit, you:

- should move the SL of the remaining order to break-even

- can choose to close the remaining order and bank roughly 50 pips profit or leave it running in the hope of catching an even larger move – this is a risk-free option as the SL is at the break-even level

From this point onward, should another trade opportunity arise while the remaining order is still open then you can take that trade (but not more than one) since half of the first trade has already been banked and the remaining half is a risk-free trade.

More Conservative Traders

1) Follow the rules laid out above, but avoid:

- opening new positions near the end of the trading day (refer to a daily chart)

- opening positions before weekends and public holidays

- trading on Fridays

More Aggressive Traders

1) Aim to risk 20% of your account equity.

For example, if available equity was $1,000:

- open a 0.40 lot position as 2 x 0.20 lot orders

- set a 25 pip TP on one order and a 45-60 pip SL on both

2) Use the approach discussed above but, after moving the SL to break-even on the remaining 0.20 lot order, you can:

- simply leave it running until it meets the conditions of Exit Strategy 2 or 3

- open additional positions, place SLs at break-even levels and leave all of them to run until they meet the conditions of Exit Strategy 2 or 3, even if this takes several days.

Again, we remind you that it is always better to close profitable positions before the weekend and major public holidays. Of course, you can leave positions open if you really want, but try to avoid opening new ones close to those times.

Update!

One thing you will discover with MetaTrader is that it is rather cumbersome to open two orders at the same entry price, with the correct SL on both and an initial TP on one of them.

Having to monitor the trades and move the SL on the remaining half of the position is also rather inconvenient as it is not always possible to sit and monitor chart movement.

For this reason, we created a semi-autotrading system, based on the 5EMAs Alert that was provided to you as part of our course package.

Amongst other things, this enhanced system automatically opens two correctly-sized orders at your command, sets SL and TP levels as appropriate and also moves the SL to break-even for you – all automatically.

The enhanced system is not only very easy to use; it is also available at a very reasonable price from the member area of the **www.EvolvedForexTrading.com** website.

REFERENCES

1. Some reference material in this publication explaining the origins of FOREX was obtained from previous versions of the Alpari Limited and MetaQuotes Software Corporation web sites.

   Alpari Limited is well known broker for FOREX and other financial instruments.

   MetaQuotes Software Corporation is the developer of the Meta Trader 4 trading platform and related products.

   Web sites:

   Alpari Limited: **www.alpari.ru**

   MetaQuotes Software Corporation: **www.metaquotes.net**

2. All other material, trading systems and other content are copyrighted developments of the authors of this book.

Printed in Great Britain
by Amazon

26435995R00134